A Time And A Season

by
James Etheridge

Edited by
Jackie Stokes

A Time And A Season
James Etheridge

If you would like to order books from the author or do any of the above, you may contact the author via AquaHue Artworks at aquahueartworks@earthlink.net

A special thanks to Mike and Lynn Gresham,
Bantes Bruce Hodges and Michael D. Ham
for their help in the publication of this book.

James Etheridge is a Georgia artist and writer. He became interested in the written word at an early age and was introduced to the modern classics in high school. He loves all style of literature, from children's books to the classics. He is a history buff as well, enjoying both biographies and historical fiction and non-fiction. His literary influences include Ernest Hemingway, Ray Bradbury, James Michener and Lewis Grizzard. James and Jackie reside in Conyers, Georgia.

Their first book, *A Place And A Time*, chronicles growing up as Baby Boomers in the suburbs of Atlanta, Georgia. *A Time And A Season* continues the memories of days gone by when doors were never locked, kids played outside until dark and everyone knew everyone else.

Reviews of *A Place And A Time*

I grew up in Marietta, Georgia and after reading the first few pages of *A Place And A Time* I thought, "This sounds familiar." And the more I read the more memories flashed back. I started thinking these stories are my stories. I played Little League. I chased foul balls and turned them in at the concession stand. I also had woods and a creek. We played Army. We explored that creek like Lewis and Clark. I had a crush on my second grade teacher. Her name was Miss Chastain. My first girlfriend worked at McDonald's. Then I realized these stories are not yours or mine. They belong to a generation. And I applaud you for writing them down.
– *Tim Burley*

I played Little League at Gresham Park and my first real job was at the Dairy Queen on Gresham Road. My first performances as a Comedy Ventriloquist and Magician were at Gresham Park. – *Mark Merchant*

I grew up in Gresham Park, at the same time. This book brought back so many memories. It really was a much easier time. Thank you for writing this book.
– *Doris McKinley*

The book is great! Even if I didn't live there or know many of the stories personally it would be a good book. – *Charlene A.*
Great stories of life and times in my era from my area.
– *H. Grant Rice*

A beautiful trip through the mid twentieth and what it was like to grow up in that time. As he writes at the end of each chapter " The memories are there. They always will be", they have been revived and enriched in his book. –*Geary F. Cagle*

This book has such a poetic flow. I enjoyed every word!
– *Jules Collins*

For Daddy,
Momma,
Poppy
and
Meme

For Bobby, Don
and the entire Cedar Grove Gang,
both with us and waiting.

And for everyone,
everywhere
who was there in
that place and time,
that time and season.

Ecclesiastes 3:1-8

Table of Contents

East Atlanta

Gresham Park is my hometown. But for the first four and-a-half years of my life and beyond, East Atlanta was and still is my original hometown. The family ties there run deep. My family is from the Auburn and Carl area, two small towns in Northeast Georgia. They are located side by side and are about five miles from Winder. My grandparents moved from there to Atlanta in the early Twenties. My aunt, my father and my two uncles were all born in East Atlanta.

The family lived on May Avenue originally and moved to Florida Avenue off of Glenwood sometime in the mid to late Thirties. My grandfather drove a delivery truck for a cleaning and laundry company before going to work for the City of Atlanta Fire Department.

When I was born, we lived at the corner of Sanders Avenue and Florida Avenue. Commenting once about my memory, Allene asked me if I remembered my birth experience. I told her that I did and it was like going down one of those big slides covered by a tube at the water park, the kind where you shoot out at the end and land in a pool of water. That's obviously not really true, but I do remember quite a few snippets of things from our house on Sanders Avenue. Like Stevey, who lived across the street. He was my first friend and was about five or six years older than me. I remember seeing him walking home from school every day. And Sherry, who for some reason we called "Nu-Nu." Her house was on Florida Avenue, three doors up from my grandparents and across from our back yard. She had dark hair, big brown eyes and we were friends right on up through our teenage years.

Our house had a big screened porch off to the side facing Florida Avenue. When I was about four, my father bought a punch-out book for me at the drug store. I don't remember what the book was about, but I remember putting it together on the porch. It's funny what sticks in the mind.

I still remember the general layout of the house. There was a bedroom to the right as you walked in the front door. The living room was to the left and the upstairs staircase was along the wall to the right. The kitchen was at the back of the house and the dining room was between it and the living room. Upstairs were two more bedrooms and at the top of the staircase was a studio that was my father's model airplane room. The back yard was big, with a swing set and a sand box. I remember having a birthday party in the back yard. I'm not sure which birthday, I just remember a large Pin The Tail On The Donkey board.

I still spent a lot of time in East Atlanta after we moved to Gresham Park. I stayed with my grandmother sometimes during the summer while my parents worked.

My grandparents' house was a small five-room house in which they raised four kids. The house had a front porch with a swing, a banister, a rocking chair and a chaise lounge with a plastic floral cover. My cousins and I played on the front porch a lot when we were there for Sunday dinners and holidays. We would climb up on the banister and walk to the corner post. We would then step around the corner post, walk to the wall of the house, turn around and walk back the same way. The banister seemed so big and so high back then.

Outside the back door was a covered porch where the big freezer sat. Back then Auburn and Carl were way out in the country and my grandparents went there often. Mema would bring fresh vegetables and fruit back from the family farms there. The farms all had lakes on them and after he retired, Pepa would go fishing at least three days a week, sometimes more. I swear that man could catch fish on dry land. Hence, the freezer was always full. I remember sitting and shelling peas with Mema on the front porch. I would snap the pods in half and hand them to her. She would open the pod and put the peas in a big pot. As I grew older, I would snap the pods, open them up and put the peas in a separate pot she had given me. When we were finished, she would take them in the kitchen and fill the pots with water and let the peas soak. She taught me how to shuck corn and peel potatoes. She had a ceramic churn that she would make butter in. When I was very young, she would let me help her churn the butter by moving the agitator stick up and down. Little kids think things like churning butter and turning the crank on the ice cream maker are a great adventure. After Mema quit using the churn and started using store-bought butter, Pepa would use the churn to ferment the muscadines and scuppernongs for his homemade wine.

Mema and Pepa's back yard was big and Pepa's garage was at the back of the property. Pepa was a serious pack rat. His garage was relatively clean, because that was where he parked his '49 Chevy Fleetline Deluxe. It sat in there for at least ten years and I never once saw or heard Pepa crank it. I have no idea what happened to it, but there is nothing that I wouldn't give to have it now. Next to the garage was the Little House, an efficiency apartment that my uncle built when he and my aunt first married. It had a Murphy bed, a sofa and a counter with stools. There was a small sink, oven, stove and a fridge behind the counter. The bathroom was off of the kitchen. I remember how it looked because at one point you could still walk in the Little House. Over time Pepa filled it up with anything and everything you can imagine. Hundreds of fishing rods, tackle boxes, bait cans, outboard motors and no telling what else was crammed in there. Eventually you could not walk in the door. You would open it and there was stuff piled as high as the ceiling. *American Pickers* would have had a field day in the Little House, if they could have ever dug their way into it.

The ice cream truck that came by Mema and Pepa's was different than the one in Gresham Park. It wasn't a truck at all, but a three-wheeled bicycle. The two wheels were in the front with the cooler in between them. The third wheel, the seat and the pedals were in the back. The handlebar was on the back of the cooler and it had little bells hanging off of it. The ice cream man had a speech impediment and no matter what you said you wanted, be it a Nutty Buddy, an Eskimo Pie or a Push-Up, he'd always ask if you wanted a Rainbow. But my cousins and me, Stevey, Nu-Nu and all the other neighborhood kids always gathered around him when he stopped. Some things are the same no matter where you might be.

I remember going into a little place called Two Points with my father. It was located at the intersection of Moreland and Flat Shoals, but it was gone by the early Sixties. The place that sticks in my mind like no other is Charlie's Place. There was an alley that ran behind Mema and Pepa's house from Sanders Avenue to Glenwood. The alley is long gone now, but back then my cousins and I would walk down the alley to Glenwood, cross the street and go into to Charlie's for candy, bubble gum and Cokes. Charlie's had hamburgers and hot dogs that would put The Varsity to shame. Charlie would soak the burgers in his special secret recipe chili, dip them out and cook them to order on the griddle. When you walked in, there was a big square counter and the kitchen was in the middle. You could watch them as they cooked. Charlie's mother worked behind the counter as well. My father would always get a dressed dog, which was a hot dog split in half on an open bun with the chili poured over the top of it. I would always get a hamburger, a Nehi chocolate drink and a pack of baseball cards.

At Glenwood and Flat Shoals, the main intersection of town, was the barbershop where I was given my first haircut. Next to that was East Atlanta Pharmacy, which had a big lunch counter. My father worked there as a soda jerk during his youth and my cousin worked there in the early Seventies delivering prescriptions. Times were very different back then. Next to the pharmacy was the appliance store where we got our first color TV, a cabinet model that was about the same size and weight of a Nash Metropolitan. Next to the appliance store was the army surplus and sporting goods store.

The army surplus store was known far and wide beyond the boundaries of East Atlanta. If you needed anything sports related, boy or girl, that was where you went. The store supplied all the high schools in the area with equipment, letter jackets, uniforms and so much more. They also carried, as the name implied, military surplus gear that pretty much entailed all four branches of service. I got my first army outfit from Archie's. It consisted of green fatigues, a helmet, an ammo belt with a clip on canteen, combat boots and insignias for the shirtsleeves. The shirt also had a white strip above the left pocket where you could write your name with a laundry marker. I was dressed and ready for Saturday afternoon maneuvers in the woods.

The last time I was in the original store was 1986. I went there to buy a pair of baseball cleats. The store moved out of East Atlanta not long after that and relocated to Stockbridge. The store is still in operation and has since moved to McDonough.

East Atlanta has since gone through a gentrification with trendy restaurants, shops and stores. The real estate is pricey, to say the least, due to the close proximity to downtown Atlanta. I looked up my grandparents' house and what it went for the last time it was sold made my jaw drop. Let's just say that it was probably more money than Pepa ever saw in his entire life.

The last time we rode through East Atlanta some guy with a backpack was riding a skateboard down Glenwood Avenue in the middle of traffic. If one of us had done that when we were kids, we would have been yelled at, run over, spanked or all of the above. The Madison Theatre is gone, along with the Texaco Station, Forrest Five and Ten, the Yum-Yum Restaurant, the A&P grocery store, the appliance store, the barber shop and the beauty parlor. The library is now a chiropractic office. John B. Gordon Elementary School and the old No. 13 Fire Station, where my father worked, have both been razed. In their place is a high-rise apartment building. A new No. 13 Fire Station has been built across the street. East Atlanta is now known as East Atlanta Village. Charlie's is completely gone, the building leveled to the ground. Seeing that put a lump in my throat the size of a chili burger. But the memories are there. They always will be.

Misty Waters

One of the most popular places to spend a summer afternoon or evening was Misty Waters Country Club. Located on Candler Road, Misty Waters was similar to the other family playgrounds that sprung up in the suburbs of the Fifties, such as Clifton Springs and Glenwood Hills. Of the three, Misty Waters was the largest.

It featured a golf course and an Olympic-sized pool with a high dive. Like Clifton Springs, there was a lake with a sand beach, a dock in the middle with a diving board and a twenty-foot platform that was two levels with a diving board at the top. There was also a miniature golf course and a roller skating rink. As a member of one of the Misty Waters social network pages said, “Where else could you play golf, swim, dance and get into a fight all in one day?”

On weekend nights the roller rink was turned into a dance hall. WQXI radio station Quixie In Dixie promoted shows there. Some of the artists who played at Misty Waters regularly were Billy Joe Royal, Joe South, Tommy Roe and Dennis Yost. Many local bands played at Misty Waters also.

I never hung out at the skating rink very much. First of all, I was too young. But the main reason was that I couldn’t skate. I couldn’t skate when I was a kid, I couldn't skate as a teenager and I can't skate now.

Like a lot of other youngsters, I took swimming lessons at Misty Waters and learned the basics with a kickboard. A couple of years later I took more lessons at Misty Waters, but by that time I could swim pretty well. As part of the final lesson we had to jump off of the high dive at the pool. Then we went up to the beach, swam out to the dock, then swam to the platform and jumped off of the high dive. There was a kid named Sherman who was afraid to go off of the high dive in the pool. I didn't know him, all I remember is that he had red hair and stood at the end of the diving board with his arms folded around his shoulders. His knees were shaking and he was crying like a baby. The instructor was in the water and kept yelling up at him that the longer he stood there, the worse he was making it. I don't think he ever jumped. The instructor finally had to go up and get him and help him back down the ladder. Sherman didn't even go to the lake and attempt to swim to the dock, let alone the platform with the high dive.

Speaking of the platform with the high dive, a few years later a group of us were there one hot Saturday in the middle of the summer. We were hanging out at the platform and one of the guys with us was afraid to go up and jump off of the top level. We finally talked him into it. He climbed unsteadily to the top, jumped off of the diving board and wracked himself when he hit the water.

He barely made it back to the platform. He staggered up the ladder and laid on the lower level flat of his back, writhing in agony. There were several girls there and we, being good friends and buddies, were laughing hysterically. The pain eventually subsided and he was able to sit up. I don't know if it was because the girls were there or what, but somehow we were able to convince him to try it again. He climbed up to the top level, jumped off of the diving board, hit the water and wracked himself again. This time the lifeguard had to swim out and get him. He towed our buddy back to the dock in the middle of the lake where he laid in a fetal position, hyperventilating. We were laughing even harder this time. Hey, what are friends for? When he was able to compose himself he climbed down the ladder, swam slowly back to the beach and refused to come into the water again. He did strike up a conversation with one of the girls from the platform, though. I think she felt sorry for him.

Misty Waters closed in the early Seventies. The lakes were filled in and an apartment complex named Misty Waters Apartments was built on the property. A friend of mine lived in the complex. I remember pulling into the complex to visit her not long after she moved there and you could still see where some of the tees and greens had been on the golf course. The apartments kept the swimming pool. It was very strange swimming there and the pool being surrounded by apartment buildings rather than the lake and the roller rink up on the hill.

The pool is gone now. The apartments are no longer called Misty Waters. I'm pretty sure you can no longer determine where the tees and greens of the golf course once were. But the memories are there. They always will be.

Rosebud

Before the development of Atlanta moved east and long before the sprawl, DeKalb County was dairy land. In the early part of the twentieth century there were at least two hundred dairy farms in the county and at least thirteen were in operation in the area south of Fayetteville and Bouldercrest Roads. In the Chamblee area of north DeKalb there were at least thirty dairy farms. DeKalb County was the largest producer of Grade A milk in the south and had more dairies than any other county in the state of Georgia.

One of the farms in particular was located on Bouldercrest Road just south of Eastland Road. It stretched all the way to just north of Key Road and Intrenchment Creek. The family that owned the farm commissioned landscape architects to design their yard and gardens. Fine shrubs, specimen trees and rows of flowers were brought in. A stone staircase, a bridge and a waterfall were built along with a ten-acre lake, complete with two islands.

After WWII the family sold the property and the garden was abandoned. Kudzu crept in, took over and covered the garden. I went fishing in the lake with my father and grandfather a few times in the Sixties and all I knew was that it was a lake in the middle of the woods off of Eastland Road. A friend and I were riding his motorcycle after school one day and wound up in the woods surrounding the lake. In the days when I was young, stupid and knew everything I would actually get on the back of a motorcycle. We were buzzing through the trees and over the trails when we rounded a corner and there in the middle of the trail stood a man with a double-barreled shotgun pointed at us. He informed us that we were on his property and we "needed to get the hell off of it right now." We complied.

In the late Nineties an abandoned apartment complex on the property was purchased and the developers began clearing the kudzu from the woods surrounding the buildings. The stone staircase, bridge and waterfall were uncovered. Landscape architects were brought in to refurbish the gardens and today the lake and the property are part of a DeKalb County public park named Emerald Lake Park.

The Gresham family owned a dairy farm that encompassed land that was to be developed into Gresham Park. Their property stretched from present day Gresham Road all the way down to a farm on Bouldercrest Road and bordered another dairy farm to the north along Flat Shoals Road. The family donated a parcel of land at Gresham Road and Clifton Church Road, which were both dirt at the time, to the county to build what would become the baseball and football fields of the Gresham Park Recreation Center.

As time passed, most of the dairy land was sold off to developers and the farms disappeared. One of the farms belonged to the family of a lifelong friend and a portion of the land became what is now I-285.

The family of a girl named Louise, with whom I grew up and went to school, owned a small farm on Gresham Road that was still there until the early two-thousands. They owned milk cows and beef cows, mostly black anguses. The farm actually belonged to her grandparents, but the family shared the land and the house she grew up in was on the property. Louise's grandfather bought the property in 1941 and her dad built their house in 1953. They all milked the cows and used the milk. The farm had a barn, a chicken house and they sold eggs and vegetables from the garden. There was also a corn crib and a smokehouse for smoking meat. Last but not least was a rabbit hutch. There was a creek on the back of the property where Louise, her brother, her sister and the neighboring kids did what all kids did back then. They played in it. Her grandparents allowed the Boy Scouts and Girls Scouts to use the land for camp-outs. The field was also used for neighborhood baseball and softball games. Louise said that she loved growing up on the farm but hated walking down Gresham Road with a milk bucket.

Puritan Dairy was located on Ward Lake Road, off of Bouldercrest Road just below the community of Cedar

Grove. It was a smaller farm and closed in the early Eighties. The old dairy building was at one time a pork rind plant and is now an incense factory. There is a convenience store and a liquor store, complete with iron bars on the doors, attached to the building. The pastureland has been paved over and in place of contented milk cows there is an auto service business, a U-Haul center and a rib shack.

The most famous of all DeKalb County dairies was Mathis Dairy. It not only survived, it thrived for decades. Mathis Dairy was located on Rainbow Drive, east of Gresham Park and became one of the most prestigious dairies in the country. R.L. Mathis started the dairy in 1917 with seventy-five acres and twelve milk cows. The dairy opened for tours and field trips in the Fifties. Mathis's mascoot was Rosebud, a beautiful honey and white Guernsey cow who patiently endured thousands of children milking her. At the end of the tour the kids would receive an *I Milked Rosebud* button, a coloring book and a small bottle of chocolate milk.

Mathis Dairy was a beautiful landmark in a country setting. There was a fountain out front as you drove up. Later on they opened up a Dairy Store at the front of the building where you could drive up and purchase milk without getting out of your car.

I would never engage in such a juvenile delinquent activity, but friends of mine used to camp out and, after a night of exploring, telling ghost stories or climbing trees would go "milking" in the early morning hours. What milking consisted of was going into a subdivision and finding a house with a Mathis Dairy delivery box on the front porch, which wasn't difficult to do. You would then sneak onto the porch, open the box and if milk had been delivered, especially chocolate milk, you would grab a bottle or two and run. After a sufficient amount of moo-juice had been pilfered, everyone would go back to camp, pull the paper stoppers out of the top of the bottles and enjoy the plunder.

Mathis Milk was available in supermarkets up until the mid-Nineties. It was available in glass gallon bottles with plastic handles and for years it was the only milk Mary Jane and I bought. You could also buy their chocolate milk in supermarkets, so my daughter knew the thrill of a long pull of the rich and smooth Mathis chocolate milk.

Mathis Dairy closed in 1995. Puritan Dairy closed in the early Eighties. The Vaughter Farm, located on Klondike Road in Lithonia, was the last working farm in DeKalb County and ceased operation in 2002. The property was sold to Panola Mountain State Park and is now part of the Arabia Mountain National Heritage Area. The large white barn is still intact and is on the Georgia Register of Historic Places.

By the time my family moved to Gresham Park the

community was largely developed and a lot of the dairy farms in the area were gone. But, I took a field trip in kindergarten to Mathis Dairy. I milked Rosebud, then she allowed forty-five other six-year-old kids lined up behind me to give her udder a squeeze or two. I got my bottle of chocolate milk, my coloring book and my *I Milked Rosebud* button. But for those who were there in that time and season when the main industry in DeKalb County was rolling pastureland, cattle in the fields and hard working families tending the farms, the memories are there. They always will be.

Pals

Besides my friends in the neighborhood, I had lots of friends in school. There was Jack, Baba Looey, Dave-O, Carl and Snuffy, to name a few. Outside of school, my friends were Herb and his older brother Eddie, Hambone and, of course, my cousin Wayne. He was a little over a year older than me and we were very close friends growing up. Wayne, my aunt and uncle and two other cousins lived right behind us in East Atlanta before we moved. They eventually moved to Gresham Park too. Wayne and I spent a lot of time at each others' houses over the years. I would spend the night at his house and he would spend the night at mine. We camped out, rode bikes, built model cars and walked to the store countless times. Wayne went to Meadowview Elementary School and I went to Gresham Park Elementary. It wasn't until high school that we went to the same school. We even had a couple of classes together.

If you wanted to go a friend's house in those days, you walked or rode your bike. I used to walk or ride to Herb and Eddie's or Wayne's all the time. Both of their houses were about a mile from ours, but it seemed a lot longer to a kid walking or pedaling a bike up and down the hills of Gresham Park in the middle of July. Come to think of it, it probably would seem a lot longer to an adult, too.

My two best friends at school were Mitch and Rick. Mitch's family moved to Gresham Park when Mitch was six, about halfway through the first grade. He was in my class and we became fast friends. His family lived on the street behind us. I could walk out of my back door, go down the hill, cross the creek, climb back up the opposite hill, cut through a side yard, take a right and I was at Mitch's front door. It took all of five minutes to walk there. Mitch's dad had chickens and a rooster. That was when you could have chickens and a rooster in DeKalb County. I can still hear that rooster crowing as I ate my breakfast and read the back of the cereal box every morning.

Mitch and I shared an affinity for drawing. We drew army men at first, then tanks, ships and airplanes. I eventually branched off into drawing hot rods, motorcycles and monsters. I usually would draw during math class and that would get me into trouble. One of my teachers had a conference with my parents and told them that I may grow up to become the next Baldy, but until then she had to teach me how to multiply and divide. Baldy was an editorial cartoonist for the Atlanta Constitution.

The teachers would put fresh paper on the bulletin board every month or so and Mitch, myself or both of us would draw the theme for the month on the board. We then started writing and drawing our own comic strips, so it was inevitable that when our class started a newspaper in the sixth grade, Mitch and I were the cartoonists. My friend Anna, who lived across the street from me, was the editor. Jack was the sports editor. All of the other students were reporters. Some submitted sports stories, others editorial and still others entertainment. Each would submit stories every week. The mom of one of the girls in our class would type up the newspaper on mimeograph paper. The school secretary would print the newspaper and it would be distributed to the class. Mitch and I were given a blank piece of mimeograph paper each week. We would block out space for six comic strips, each drawing three apiece. Mitch did the *How Come Dept.* and I did *Grin and Laugh At It.* Those are the only two that I can recall.

Rick and I became friends in the third grade. The third grade was the first year we were separated into blocs and each class remained basically the same until we graduated after the seventh grade. One of the first things I remember about Rick was the two of us doing a puppet show together. The whole class paired up and did skits, using the teacher's desk as the stage. We created our own scripts and Rick and I did ours about football. The storyline long escapes me, but I remember each of our puppets were in green and white uniforms. This was due to the fact that the team I played on at Gresham Park was the Wasps and our colors were green and white. My mother made the puppets on her sewing machine.

Rick and I both loved the outdoors and would tell each other about our after-school hikes and explorations at school the following morning. Rick also whetted my appetite for reading and writing, James Bond in particular. He had a copy of *Goldfinger*, which he lent to me after he had finished it. I read it and then went with my cousin Wayne to see the movie at the Madison Theatre. It was the first grown-up movie that either of us had ever seen. Rick and I then began trying to write our own spy novels on notebook paper and were convinced that we were going to send them in to Signet Publishers when they were finished. We also began writing stories of two spies of the reptilian persuasion, Leonard Leech and Luke Lizard. The femme fatale of the stories was Sabra Scorpion. Leonard and Luke's archenemy was the Smelly Old Three-Toed Sloth.

Much to my parents' chagrin, Rick also turned me on to The Smothers Brothers. In the sixth grade, we each had to write a story and tell it out loud to the class. Rick paraphrased a version of the famous *Mom Always Liked You Best* routine. I went out and bought a copy of the *Golden Hits of the Smothers Brothers* album and started watching their Sunday evening TV show. My father was not amused. One day I went home after school with my friend Snuffy. His last name was Smith, so that's why we called him Snuffy. He put on his older brother's Bill Cosby album *I Started Out As A Child*. That was all it took for me. I bought five or six of Cosby's albums and memorized all of them verbatim. Occasionally the teacher would let me stand up in front of the class and deliver one of Cosby's routines. My mother used to ask me why I could remember a whole Bill Cosby album but couldn't remember my math homework. I would shrug my shoulders and say, "Well, math's not funny."

Mitch and I went through high school together, but Rick moved away and went to Southwest DeKalb after we graduated from Gresham Park Elementary School. He went on to become an All-State fullback, helping lead the Panthers to the State AA Championship in '72. He then played college football at Appalachian State University. I played football for five years at Walker. I made it as high as a backup center and played on the kickoff and kickoff return teams. I saw Rick on the field after we played SWD our senior year. I shook his hand, congratulated him and wished him luck for the rest of the season. That was the last time I saw him. I am sure Rick has done well. He had a way about him that everyone liked.

I have managed to stay in touch with Mitch's family, more so than Mitch himself. His sisters are art directors in the advertising business, as was my late wife, Mary Jane. They worked together at various points in time. His younger brother has the artistic gene as well, creating incredible pen and ink works. Mitch graduated from Georgia Tech with a degree in Architectural

Engineering and moved to Columbia, South Carolina. I slacked off for five years after high school before going to DeKalb Technical College and studying commercial art, then landing a job, ironically, in the art department at the Atlanta Journal and Constitution.

I saw Mitch at one of our high school reunions a few years back. We ran into each other at the bar. We bought each other a drink. We both kept slapping each other on the shoulder and saying how great it was to see one another again. I told him how I had drawn a series of comic strips and tried to get them syndicated. He laughed and said, "You and I never drew any comic strips together, did we?" We both had a big laugh at that. The memories are there. They always will be.

Ooey Gooey

"Hey, gang, it's time for the Popeye Club!" These were words that kids everywhere in Atlanta heard on TV every weekday at 5pm. *The Popeye Club* was a children's TV show hosted by Officer Don that aired on WSB Channel 2 from 1956 until 1970. Officer Don was the affable neighborhood City Of Atlanta policeman, complete with a badge and a whistle on a braided lanyard, which he would blow loud and often. Don Kennedy, a booth announcer for WSB, portrayed him. My mother said that he was silly, which was exactly why kids loved him.

Live and local television programming was the norm back then and featured cooking shows, quiz shows and variety shows. *The Popeye Club* was screened before a live studio audience made up of about thirty-five kids and was originally called *The Clubhouse Gang*. The name was changed to *The Popeye Club* sometime in the early Sixties, but Officer Don still referred to the kids in the audience as the "Gang." The hour-long show became a huge hit. It was aired from WSB TV's studios at the White Columns On Peachtree building from five until six every weekday afternoon. The waiting list to get on the show was about a year.

Officer Don led the kids in games such as musical chairs, wheelbarrow races and untie the knot. But by far the most famous and most remembered game was something called Ooey Gooey. The premise was simple. Officer Don would place three sacks filled with goodies on a Lazy Susan sitting atop a small table. In the fourth sack, he would mix up a concoction made up of such materials as mud, raw eggs, chocolate syrup, ketchup and honey. This was the Ooey Gooey bag. He would then pick a kid out of the audience, blindfold him or her and spin the Lazy Susan until the kid told him to stop. Officer Don would invariably ask the contestant if they were sure that was where they wanted to stop. The kid would take the bait and continue or take a chance on where the bags had stopped spinning, then stick their hand into the bag and find either goodies or Ooey Gooey. If they found the Ooey Gooey bag, the Gang would laugh and yell "OOOOOEY GOOOOEY!" The hapless contestant would then go off camera to wash their hands and Officer Don gave them a goodie bag when they returned.

If a kid was lucky enough to get on the show on his or her birthday, Officer Don would first ask who had a birthday on that particular day. The birthday kids would raise their hands and he would talk to each one individually on camera. He would ask them their name, how old they were and what they wanted to be when they grew up. If a kid said they wanted to be a TV cameraman, Officer Don would send them over to Uncle Ray, the lead cameraman. Uncle Ray would let them stand on the platform, hold the controls and look through the viewfinder. One of the other cameras would pan around and show the kid at the camera with Uncle Ray. Officer Don always referred to the crew as "Uncle." Uncle Aubrey was up in the booth. You never saw Uncle Aubrey.

And, of course, there were the cartoons. The show was aired in black and white at first and the cartoons were mostly the old Fleischer *Popeye* cartoons with Popeye, Bluto, Olive Oyl, Wimpy, Alice The Goon and Eugene The Jeep. Eventually the show began broadcasting in color and the cartoons shifted to color *Popeye* cartoons and others such as *Krazy Kat, Snuffy Smith* and *Beetle Bailey.* Officer Don would always select a kid out of the audience to help with the "Cartoon Countdown." He and the kid would count down with their fingers and shout, "Five, Four, Three, Two, One!" accompanied by The Clubhouse Gang.

In the mid-Sixties a character was introduced which became the undeniable star of the show. He was a green dragon arm puppet worked by a young Atlanta puppeteer named Terry Kelley. His name was Orville The Dragon. He quickly became the comedian with Officer Don as the straight man. Orville could convince the naive Officer Don into falling for anything, be it a pie in the face, an exploding birthday cake or getting pelted with ping-pong balls. Orville became so popular he began hosting other kids' TV shows on Saturday mornings.

I was lucky enough to be on the show in 1965 when I was ten years old. I was with my Cub Scout den and it was an experience I remember vividly to this day. My den mother picked us all up after school and we rode downtown in her station wagon. We got a tour of White Columns and then waited at the top of the stairs, which led down to the studio. I remember when Officer Don came out to lead us downstairs. It was the first time I had ever seen anyone famous in person. I remember the studio being very dark. We climbed the stairs that led to the soundproof booth that was located on the ceiling at the right-hand side of the studio. It had rows of folding theatre seats in it and this was where the parents sat while the show was being aired. In the studio there was a TV monitor hanging from the ceiling where the cartoons were shown. My den mates and I were wearing our Cub Scout uniforms and the game we played was, of course, Ooey Gooey. None of us were picked to play, but I do remember that the kid that did play got Ooey Gooey, so we did get to shout "OOOOOEY GOOOOEY!" At the end of the show every one of us in The Clubhouse Gang got a goody bag. Officer Don plugged all of the contents of the goody bag at the end of the show, undoubtedly sponsors. I think that the local chapter of the Atlanta Federation of Dentists was also a major sponsor.

The show also featured local talent from young performers. A longtime of mine, a ventriloquist and magician who later became a professional entertainer, performed on the show several times. The last time I remember watching *The Popeye Club* was when I was about twelve years old. A local Gresham Park band called The Night Riders appeared on the show. The band was made up of guys that we all knew and the songs that they played on the show were *In The Midnight Hour* and *Louie, Louie.* After they played, Officer Don talked with them just like Ed Sullivan and The Beatles on The Ed Sullivan Show.

The Popeye Club ran for fourteen seasons on WSB TV. It is the longest-running kids' show in Atlanta television history and was, at one time, the highest-rated kids' show in the nation. The show was so popular that when it switched to color RCA used it as a test market for some of their very first color television cameras.

The Popeye Club is gone now, as are other mainstays of the era of live Atlanta TV such as *Bestoink Dooley's Big Movie Shocker, Tubby and Lester, Mr. Pix, Buddy Farnan's Magic Funnies* and *Dialing For Dollars*, all replaced by *Minecraft, Fortnite* and *Grand Theft Auto,* which is a good game for kids to be playing. Even *Live Atlanta Wrestling* is gone, though it continued into the Eighties as *Georgia Championship Wrestling.* The matches were taped on Saturday mornings at the WTBS studio on West Peachtree Street and aired on Saturday and Sunday evenings. *Georgia Championship Wrestling* was bought out in the mid-Eighties by the nationally syndicated *World Championship Wrestling*, marking the end of live-television programming in Atlanta, in Georgia and in the South. But the memories are there. They always will be.

The Caped Crusader

In January 1966 a TV show hit the airwaves on ABC that became a national phenomenon. *Batman* aired for the first time and quickly became one of the most popular shows in the history of television. Based on the *Batman* comic books, the TV series was colorful, campy, satiric and funny, nothing like the dark and mysterious tone of the comic books. It aired from '66 through '68.

As a ten-year-old kid, I was hooked. We immediately began to play Batman in the neighborhood. The only problem was that everybody wanted to be Batman or Robin. Nobody wanted to be a bad guy like the Joker, the Penguin or the Riddler. The little girl who lived next door wanted to be Catwoman. But she didn't want to be a villain either, so we made up situations and dramas where we would save Gresham Park from being taken over by maniacal supercrooks intent on certain doom and destruction. We would foil the Joker from blowing up the ballpark or the Riddler from poisoning Gresham Park's drinking water. We would stop the Penguin from taking over the Atlanta Airport. City Hall would eventually take over the Atlanta Airport and I seriously doubt if a couple of kids dressed up in makeshift superhero outfits could have prevented that from happening.

Our basement was the Batcave. We didn't have any

Batpoles to slide down, so when Commissioner Gordon called on the Batphone, which was a red toy phone that once had belonged to Brain's little sister, we had to run out of my room and down the stairs to the Batcave. The only catch was we couldn't change into our Batsuits halfway down the stairs, so we had to be dressed and ready for action when a crisis arose.

I had a little black Briggs & Stratton T-Model when I was growing up, one like the Shriners drove in the parades. That was our Batmobile. It didn't have fins or bubble windows and was definitely not turbine powered, but it was black with red seats and worked perfectly for a couple of nine-year-old kids. Besides, it was power driven and was better than rigging up a cardboard box and pretending to blast around Gresham Park. I'm sure the two of us in our masks, capes and gloves riding around the yard in a miniature T-Model doing battle with dastardly villains must have been a sight to behold.

Batman was cool, but I liked Robin. He was closer to our age, or so we thought. He went to school during the day and out on patrol with Batman at night. He wore a cool red costume, green tights and gloves, a yellow cape and a black mask. I knew this because one of my father's model airplane buddies had a color TV. Daddy took me over to his house one night so I could watch *Batman* in color. It was quite a thrill. My mother made a Robin outfit for me on her sewing machine. I drew a picture of how it looked, she took it from there and created an almost perfect replica of the Boy Wonder's crime-fighting suit. I wore it Trick or Treating that Halloween. Since I was Robin and owned the Batmobile, I drove and Batman rode shotgun. That was okay because we were saving the world, which to us at the time was Gresham Park.

There was a contest at the local Big Apple grocery store where you could "Win An Evening With Batman." We all entered it and eagerly awaited the results. In the meantime the speculation went wild. My cousin and I wondered what the itinerary for the evening would be. The way we figured it, you would first get to visit stately Wayne Manor with Bruce Wayne and Dick Grayson and see where they played three-dimensional chess. You would get to meet Alfred the Butler and Bruce's Aunt Harriet and then slide down the Batpoles. Batman and Robin would be in the Batcave by that time and give you the full tour. Then you would get to go out on patrol with them. Never mind that the Batmobile only had two seats and you would have to ride crammed in behind them. That was never taken into consideration.

As it turned out we couldn't have been more wrong and my cousin found that out firsthand. His next-door neighbor won the contest. Unbeknownst to us, Big Apple had been staging the contest all over town and the grand prize from each store turned out to be two free tickets to a nighttime screening of the 1943 film *The Batman*. My cousin's next-door neighbor invited him to go. All I remember my cousin telling me about the movie was that it was in black and white and Batman and Robin were battling some Japanese guy.

A year later in 1967 the real Caped Crusader made a movie and they pulled out all the stops. Batman's four archenemies, the Joker, the Riddler, the Penguin and Catwoman were in the movie. They were, of course, trying to take over the world and Batman and Robin used every cool Bat-means of Transportation in their arsenal to bring their foes to bay. Besides the Batmobile, which in my humble opinion is the greatest Batmobile ever, they employed the Batboat, the Batcopter, the Batcycle and the Batplane. The only thing they didn't use was the Batsnowmobile. Of course, they triumphed in the end and the evil quartet was brought to justice. I saw the movie by myself on a weekday afternoon at the Madison in East Atlanta. My mother dropped me off and there was hardly anyone in the theatre. After the movie I walked to my grandparents' house. It was the first time I had ever been to the movies alone.

Like all crazes and fads, Batman began to fade by the following year. By then my interests had shifted to cars, football and girls, not necessarily in that order. The television series was cancelled in the spring of 1968. But for one glorious year we went to school during the day and battled supervillains in the afternoon and on weekends. We kept the good citizens of Gresham Park safe from the plots and capers of the Joker, the Riddler and the Penguin. We were all safe from Catwoman because she wasn't a villainess in Gresham Park. She was the little girl next door. The memories are there. They always will be.

Penny Loafers

When I was about nine or ten years old, my mother took me to Shoetown on Candler Road and I got my first pair of penny loafers. When we got home the first thing I did was run into my room and grab my Baba Looey bank. I took his big plastic hat off, fished out a couple of pennies and slipped them into the slits on the front of the shoes. I was thrilled and could not wait until school Monday to wear my new penny loafers and show them off. So I didn't wait. I washed the car, earned my dollar and headed up to the store wearing my stylish new footwear.

Before I left the house I made a decision that made a profound and lasting impression on me. The fashion trend at the time was penny loafers, Bass Weejuns to be precise, with no socks. All the cool teenagers wore them that way. I wasn't a teenager yet, but I was definitely cool now that I had a new pair of penny loafers. I put on my surfer shirt with no collar, pulled on my Sears camping shorts, slipped my new shoes onto my bare feet and headed out the door and down the driveway.

About halfway up the hill on Rollingwood Lane, my feet began to feel hot and the backs of my ankles were beginning to get sore. When I got to the top of the hill I sat down on the curb and took my shoes off. My big toes and little toes were beginning to get red but weren't too bad so I figured that it was safe to continue. I walked down Flintwood Drive and took the shortcut through the back yard of the supposedly mean man with the supposedly mean dog that he would supposedly sic on you and then shoot at you as you ran across the yard. I had never seen any mean man or any dog in the back yard but still ran as fast as I could every time I crossed it. I figured it was better to be safe than sorry.

By the time I ran across the yard, jumped the fence, followed the path through the woods and came out on Vicki Lane my feet were killing me. I sat down on the curb and took off my new penny loafers. Both of my big toes had big blisters on the sides of them, as did my little toes. The backs of my heels were completely raw where the leather had rubbed against my Achilles tendons. I let them air out for a few minutes, slipped the shoes back on and continued gamely on my way.

I did not make it far, only about two or three doors down before I crossed the street and sat down on the curb beside the Gulf station. I took my shoes off and decided to walk barefoot. The bottoms of my feet were tough as leather from a summer of going barefoot, but my poor upper feet were not prepared for the abuse they had just been put through. I walked up the sidewalk on Gresham Road, carrying my new penny loafers past the Standard station and turned left into the 7-Eleven store. There was no way I was carrying my shoes inside, lest I saw someone I knew, so I sat down on the curb and eased my shoes back on, wincing and grimacing.

I bought a medium cola Slurpee and four or five packs of Bazooka bubble gum. Sitting on the curb outside the store, I took my shoes off, drank my Slurpee and read a couple of Bazooka Joe comics from the bubble gum packs. I waited for a while, hoping someone from the neighborhood would pull in with their mom or dad so I could get a ride home. After a while I stood up to leave and suddenly had a brilliant idea. I gingerly slipped my shoes back on, went into the store and bought a small Slurpee. Sitting on the curb outside, I took my shoes off again and poured the ice cold frozen drink over my toes and heels. It felt cool, soothing and I let it soak on my feet for a few minutes. I held on to the hope that someone I knew would pull up for a Slurpee, but no one did. I eventually gave up hope, wiped my feet down with a paper napkin, stood up and began the long trek home.

I had slipped my new penny loafers back on, hoping that the Slurpee bath had helped. It hadn't. By the time I got back to the Gulf station, not only did my feet feel like they were on fire, they were also all sticky inside of my shoes. I sat down on the curb and took off the shoes. It was obvious now that I was going to have to walk the rest of the way home barefoot. Turning up Vicki Lane, I walked up to where the path went into the woods for the shortcut, followed it to the chain link fence and climbed over. The metal wire felt like knives on the raw spots of my toes and my teeth were gritted in agony. Dropping down into the cool grass of the back yard, I stood for a few minutes and let the balm of cool, shady turf ease my burning feet.

No supposedly mean dog came after me. No supposedly mean man came out with a double-barreled shotgun either, so I crossed the yard. I didn't sprint this time. I didn't even trot, instead walking slowly and feeling the cool grass between my toes. I reached the gate and opened it, walked down the side yard and headed back up Flintwood toward Rollingwood. I thought briefly about stopping at The Girl's house, but then realized that I would have to stand in the driveway and talk to her through the screen door. There was no way I could look cool while holding my penny loafers with my feet all swollen, raw, sticky and red, so I headed down Rollingwood toward home.

I walked through front yards and the therapeutic comfort of fescue whenever I could. Even weeds were a welcome relief. But when I got to the bottom of the hill, front yards, fescue and weeds were no longer an option. Past Bubba-Bubba's house and all the way up to ours was nothing but asphalt. I thought about crossing the street and walking through Anna's front yard and her perfectly manicured Bermuda grass, but that would be walking with the traffic and I was taught never to do that.

Suddenly I had a wonderful idea, a much better idea than walking to the store in new penny loafers with no socks. I cut across the football field on Bubba-Bubba's side yard, tiptoed gingerly across the rocks on the creek bank and stepped in. I stood there for what seemed like an eternity, letting the cold water flow over my pods, between my toes and up my heels. I walked slowly up the creek and through the woods all the way up to our back yard. I stepped carefully, avoiding rocks and walking through the sand at the bottom of the creek bed. Climbing the hill and crossing the back yard, I was never more thankful for all of the work my father had put into making the beautiful green grass grow. I vowed never to grumble about mowing the lawn again.

I went into the house and made my way to my room. My penny loafers were still clean and shiny, which was not surprising since I had carried them most of the way. I did not want my mother to see my feet because I was certain that she would see them, flip out and take me up to see Aunt Hurricane. Aunt Hurricane was the pediatrician in Gresham Park. I loved Aunt Hurricane, but I was embarrassed to tell her my feet looked like hamburger meat because I had walked to the store in penny loafers with no socks.

I put the penny loafers in my closet, went into the bathroom and ran a tub of cold water. Locking the door behind me, I sat on the edge of the tub with my feet in the water until the swelling went down and the throbbing subsided. I toweled them off and surveyed the damage. There were two blisters on each big toe, one at the top and one on the inside. My two little toes had one each on the outside and my heels each had a big raw spot on the back. I put Blistex on the affected areas, wrapped my toes and covered each heel with Band-Aids and pulled on a pair of socks. I then hobbled back to my bedroom, turned on the little black and white television, fell on my bed and watched *Rin Tin Tin*. I never wore penny loafers without socks again. The memories are there. They always will be.

You Meet The Nicest People

Honda pretty much cornered the light motorcycle market in the Sixties. They were clean, light, dependable and affordable. They became a cultural craze, just like sidewalk surfing, Slurpees and Super Balls. Their advertising slogan was *You Meet The Nicest People On a Honda* and they sold millions of bikes in the United States alone.

My mother's best friend in the neighborhood and her husband lived one street over. Their son was a few years older than me and both of my parents thought that he had hung the moon. He had a Honda 90 and my parents and I were over for dinner at their house one Saturday evening. He took me for a ride on it. It was the first time I had ever ridden on a motorcycle and after that I wanted a Honda so bad I could taste it. Not long after that a big kid up the street bought a black Honda 50. One afternoon I was outside with my friend Billy in his front yard. The big kid stopped by and offered to give me a ride up the street. I climbed on the back and my old man immediately came running out of our basement door, purple as an onion, screaming, waving his arms and chewing nails. I jumped off the back and he stood there in the middle of the street, screaming at me in front of my friends and the whole world that if I ever got on one of those blankity-blank things again he was going to stomp a mud hole in my [gluteus maximus]. It certainly didn't make it any easier when Billy climbed on the back of the bike, looked at me and laughed, waved bye-bye and motored off up the street with the big kid.

I soon found out why I was not allowed to get anywhere near a motorcycle. My uncle told me it was because my father had wrecked a 1937 Indian Scout when he was thirteen years old. Daddy worked as a soda jerk at East Atlanta Pharmacy. One of his buddies owned the Scout and Daddy rode it home for lunch one day. On the way back to work, he pulled out of Ormewood Avenue onto Gresham Avenue and into the path of an oncoming car. The car hit him broadside, tore up the bike, literally knocked him cross-eyed and ended my chances of ever owning a motorcycle until I was old enough to buy one of my own. It wasn't the car's fault and it certainly wasn't my father's fault for pulling out in front of the car. It was the motorcycle's fault. Never mind that a thirteen- year-old kid should just be graduating from a Huffy to a Schwinn Flyer and not climbing onto an Indian Scout. That didn't matter. Motorcycles became death traps with saddlebags and handlebar streamers.

But apparently it all depended on who owned the motorcycle. A few years later we were invited to dinner again one evening at the kid's house who lived one street over. He had traded in his Honda 90 for a 300 Dream, just like the one Elvis rode in the movie *Roustabout.* He asked me if I wanted to go for a ride. I looked anxiously at my father and he didn't flip out. As a matter of fact, he didn't say anything at all. I pulled on the helmet, hopped on the back of the bike and hoped we could get out of the driveway and up the street before he went ballistic and started chasing us, spouting profanities. We made it up the street all right and went for about a thirty-minute ride around Gresham Park. I was in heaven and never wanted the ride to end. When we pulled back into the driveway and went into the house, my father never even looked up at us and simply continued on with the adult conversation in the living room. So it was okay to ride with the kid one street over but not the big kid up the street. Even at that young age the double standard was not lost on me.

My father loved airplanes. He built model planes from childhood through the rest of his life. He raced in control-line competitions in the Fifties and early Sixties and won quite a number of trophies and titles along the way. He began taking flying lessons in the spring of 1963 at Gunn Air Field on Panola Road in Lithonia. One of the firemen Daddy worked with owned a Cessna 180 and kept it at Gunn. The fireman's name was Meathouse. That was all I ever heard him called and all I ever knew him by. One day my father picked me up after school and took me out to Gunn. On the way he told me that we were going to go for a ride with Meathouse in his Cessna. He also stressed that under no circumstances was I to breathe a word of it to my mother. We went up twice. The second time I got to sit up front and Meathouse let me have the control wheel by myself for a couple of minutes. It was one of the greatest thrills of my life. We flew over dairy farms, fields and Stone Mountain. I couldn't wait to get to school the next day and tell my friends all about it.

After I was grown, Daddy told me that at supper on the day that we went up in Meathouse's Cessna, I held my fingers about a quarter of an inch apart and asked my mother, "Momma, did you know that from way up in the air a man on a tractor only looks this big?" It didn't happen at the table or in front of me but apparently she had a conniption. He said that she let him know in no uncertain terms it was perfectly okay for him to kill himself but not me. When he told me that it all fell into place. In the years following when we would go to the airport either at Gunn or Stone Mountain Airport, where other friends of Daddy's had planes, we never went for a ride. I would ask him when we were going to go up again and never got much of an answer.

At the Southeastern Fair that fall my father and I went up in a Bell 47 Helicopter, like the one on the TV show *Whirlybirds*. My mother stood on the ground and watched. After the ride the pilot gave me a pair of wings and a card certifying me as a Whirlybird Co-Pilot. Both stayed on the bulletin board in the kitchen for years. So as far as my mother was concerned, it was perfectly okay for me to fly in a whirlybird with my father and certainly okay later on to fly in an airliner to visit her family in Dallas. But absolutely under no circumstances was I ever again to go up with him in Meathouse's Cessna. And as far as my father was concerned, it was perfectly okay for me to go flying in an airplane or a whirlybird, but I had better not even smell the exhaust fumes of a motorcycle, unless the kid who lived one street over was driving. And all that did was make me want a Honda even more. The yearning turned into full-blown covetousness. I saved up my yard-cutting and car-washing dollars for a Vrroom motor from the dime store. I put it on my orange Stingray bike, painted cardboard tubes silver and rigged them up with hose clamps to make an exhaust pipe just like the one on the big kid's Honda 50. I cut up an old white belt and bolted it onto the banana seat for a seat strap, which actually became functional. The exhaust pipes disintegrated one day on the way home from school in the rain, the Vrroom motor broke after a few months, but the strap was bolted on tight and was good for holding things while you rode.

When I was seventeen my dream finally came true. My friend Kurney gave me a blue 1966 Honda 50. It didn't run because it needed a battery and a clutch. I didn't care. It was a Honda and I finally had one. I took it home and parked it in the basement. I would sit on it while I talked on the phone with the long cord. I was over the moon. I had a friend at school named Crow

who knew everything there was to know and more about motorcycles. I asked him if he could get a clutch and a battery and help me install them. About a week later I came home from school and the Honda was gone. I ran upstairs where I found my father sitting at the kitchen table drinking coffee and smoking Lucky Strikes. I demanded to know what had happened to my motorcycle. "Oh, I sold it to Crow for fifty dollars," he said. "You did what?" I yelled.
"He came by with a clutch and a battery. He said you told him he could have it, you didn't want it anymore."
"I didn't tell him that! He was only going to help me get it running!"
"Well that's what he said. He got it running and rode it home. He said he's going to make a chopper out of it."

When I got to school the next morning the first thing I did was hunt Crow down and told him what my father had told me. "I didn't tell him that," said Crow. "He told me that you said you didn't want it and offered to sell it to me for fifty bucks." I believed Crow and never saw one penny of the fifty dollars. It took me a long time to get over that one. I'm not sure if I really ever did.

A similar situation happened about ten years later. A friend of mine gave me a beat up Cyclops Mini-Bike sometime in the mid-Seventies. It sat in the basement for years and Daddy finally restored it. It was beautiful. It had a new seat, a new blue paint job, new foot pegs and grips and a shiny rebuilt 3.5 HP Briggs & Stratton engine. Then it sat in the basement and nobody ever rode it. I'm not sure if it was ever even cranked after he had finished it. I made the comment that I'd like to take it over to my house and take my three-year-old daughter for rides up and down the street. He sold it the next day.

I finally got my hands on a Honda 550 Four when I moved out of the house and my father informed me very loudly that I "did not possess the intellectual capacity the Good Lord gave a burro," only not in those exact words. Then he almost tore the door to the basement off the hinges before storming downstairs to smoke half a pack of Luckies. My mother jumped in with both feet, too. She called me a day later and told me that our insurance agent said that there was no way he could insure me on a motorcycle. I knew that it wasn't true because I had already talked to him. All he told me was to be careful, but I didn't tell her that. I told her that was fine, I'd go to Allstate. My father got on the phone then and again I was informed that I did not possess the intellectual capacity the Good Lord gave a burro, then hung up on me. I went with Allstate and out for a ride.

All these years later, I still want a Honda. Not just any Honda, but one of the Sixties models I grew up coveting. Maybe I'll get one some day. Probably not. But if I ever do, I'm going to put on my father's old leather Navy flight jacket. I may look like Elvis in the Fat Years, but I won't care. I'm going to climb on, kick start the motor and take Daddy and myself for a long ride in the country, blissfully lacking the intellectual capacity the Good Lord gave a burro. The memories are there. They always will be.

Six Flags

It was my eighteenth birthday, June 26, 1973, a Tuesday to be exact. I was on a date with Patricia Perfect. That was really her name and it fit her to a tee. I picked her up after work and we headed west on I-20 from South DeKalb to Austell and Six Flags Over Georgia. That was when you could get from South DeKalb to Six Flags in thirty minutes at five in the afternoon. We headed straight for the Lickskillet section and The Great American Scream Machine.

The Scream Machine was in its first year of operation and was at the time the world's tallest, longest and fastest roller coaster. The Scream Machine is a classic wooden coaster, built along the lines of the Starliner in Panama City and the Cyclone on Coney Island. The line was long and we were in the queue house for about half an hour. Up in one of the corners was a closed-circuit television set with an animated stick character. The TV was hooked up to a remote camera and someone was watching the queue line and talking to the patrons, but it appeared that the cartoon stick character was talking because his eyes and lips moved. This was cutting-edge technology for the time. The stick figure had kind of a nasally voice and was not afraid of hurling insults. As we passed under the set, he asked Patricia what brought her to Six Flags on such a fine evening. She told him that we were there for my birthday. He wanted to know how old I was and I told him eighteen. He made some sort of snide comment about me being a young whippersnapper and if he could get out of that TV set he'd take her away from me.

When we reached the front of the line and moved out on to the platform to board the next coaster, we were told to go and stand on the number one dot. "They're putting us in the very front car. Are you okay with that?" I said to Patricia.
"I'm okay with it, are you okay with it?" she replied.
"Sure, I'm okay with it. "
"Have you ever ridden on the front of a roller coaster before?"
"Oh, yeah, I've ridden on the front of The Dahlonega Mine Train."
I looked out at the massive lift hill of The Scream Machine and something told me that The Dahlonega Mine Train was mere child's play compared to this. In reality I was scared to death, but I couldn't let Patricia know it.

The coaster pulled into the station, stopped, unloaded and we climbed in the front car. They pulled the lap bars down over our waists and we rolled out of the station toward the lift hill. There was no turning back now. At the bottom of the lift the chain grabbed the coaster, jerked it forward and we clanked and moaned up the lift hill. The higher we climbed the more my heart was pounding. The chain let go and we went over the top. When you are looking at The Scream Machine's lift hill from the ground the drop does not look that intimidating. When you go over the top in the front car it looks like you are going straight down. And don't let anyone tell you that when you are in the front car the cars behind you have to catch up. That may be true on The Dahlonega Mine Train, but when you are on The Scream Machine, you drop down the lift hill and you are flying. I've ridden a lot of roller coasters in my time, but that initial ride with Patricia Perfect in the front car of The Great American Scream Machine is the one that sticks out in my mind more than any other.

By the time Six Flags Over Georgia opened in 1967, I was already a seasoned Six Flags veteran. My mother was from Dallas, Texas and we spent summers there throughout my youth. The first time we went to Six Flags Over Texas was in 1962. One of the things I remember most is The Tree Slide, which was a tall fiberglass tree with a circular slide on the inside. You climbed a spiral staircase around the tree and the slide entrance was at the very top. The slide went in a circular motion all the way to the bottom of the tree, where you came out at the trunk. I know it seems tame by today's standards, but for a seven-year-old kid it was quite a thrill.

My older cousin and I rode on The Humble Happy

Motoring Freeway. The ride consisted of small go-cart sized vehicles with sport car bodies. Each car was powered with a seven-and-a-half horsepower rear gas engine. The cars traveled around the track at six miles per hour, passing Happy Motoring billboards and waving by-passers. The roadway contained a thick metal guide-strip directly in the middle. The guide-strip prevented the cars from leaving the track while still allowing the driver to steer the car. My cousin was twelve and he drove. We both thought we were riding on a real, full-sized freeway. The only difference in The Happy Motoring Freeway and the freeways of today is that there was no gridlock, no knuckleheads on crotch rockets weaving in and out of traffic and no road rage.

As I grew into adulthood, I came to appreciate exactly what my parents, aunts and uncles went through for us kids on the trips to Six Flags. The park was open from ten in the morning until ten at night and we would stay the entire day. Sure, there were lots of things that the adults could enjoy, but it was mostly for the kids. And our group was pretty large, too. There were about fifteen of us in all. I can't imagine going with that many people and spending twelve hours at an amusement park in the middle of summer in Dallas. But they did, and I am grateful for it. As a youngster, the trip to Dallas and Six Flags was the highlight of the year.

When Six Flags Over Georgia was built the park opened

its gates for a walk-through in the fall of 1966. My parents and I went there for the guided tour. None of the rides were operating and a number of them were still under construction. The Log Flume, one of the premier and most enduring rides of the Six Flags franchise was already built and undergoing tests. The Runaway Mine Train, which opened that spring at Six Flags Over Texas and was the premier roller coaster ride at the park, was also featured at Six Flags Over Georgia and re-named The Dahlonega Mine Train. This was heady stuff for an eleven-year-old kid. Six Flags was coming to Atlanta!

One of my favorite rides at Six Flags Over Texas was something called The Spee-Lunkers Cave. The entrance to the ride was a fiberglass rock formation. Patrons floated in a canal through the cave in fiberglass tubs made to look like wooden ones. The cave was inhabited by Spee-Lunkers, which were animated creatures with big eyes, pointed ears and long, pointed noses. They were engaged in such activities as playing music, tossing a boulder back and forth over the canal and flying a kite in a storm. The canal then went through a large tube, which rotated right to left and gave the riders the feeling and illusion that the tub was turning over. The ride was very dark, illuminated with black lights and was a welcome relief from the Texas summer heat. During the tour of Six Flags Over Georgia, I asked the guide if the Cave ride was going to be there. She assured me that it would. I was thrilled. When we arrived for our initial visit to the park in the summer of '67 the Cave ride was indeed in operation. But there were no Spee-Lunkers inside. Instead it was inhabited by Uncle Remus characters and called the Tales Of The Okefenokee. I was devastated.

The last time I was at Six Flags was in the summer of '92. My wife Mary Jane and I took my daughter and her friend there for the day. For some reason there were elephant rides going on outside the gate. My daughter, her friend and I climbed up the ladder and onto the elephant's back. My daughter became frightened and started screaming her head off. The attendant climbed the ladder, took her down and her friend and I rode the elephant around in circles for about ten minutes. When the attendant stopped the elephant we dismounted, climbed down the ladder and I crossed one off of The Bucket List. Later on that day, we went to see the dolphin show featuring Skipper and Dolly. At the finale, Skipper and Dolly swam very fast in a circle around the pool, jumped high and slapped the water with their tails, splashing a section of the audience, which just happened to be the section where we were sitting. My daughter, her friend and Mary Jane all got soaked. I was sitting right next to them and did not get one drop on me, which I found to be quite humorous. Mary Jane, however, did not.

Before Six Flags was there Funtown. Funtown was

located on Stewart Avenue and in addition to the amusement park there was a bowling alley and a miniature golf course. The amusement park featured miniature boat rides, a car ride similar to the Happy Motoring Freeway at Six Flags, large spinning teacups and a roller coaster called the Wild Mouse. The Wild Mouse was the feature ride at Funtown and was a low-speed roller coaster characterized by tight turns and one-hundred-eighty-and-degree spins. The cars were small, seated four and the wheels were situated under the riders so that when the car approached the turn it gave the impression that the car was going to continue straight and plunge off the track. I only went to Funtown a couple of times. My mother took me once and we road the little boats and the miniature train but not the Wild Mouse. I begged her but she wouldn't get on it. I finally got to ride it when one of my older cousins from Dallas came for a visit and the two of us went to Funtown. I was afraid to tell her we rode The Wild Mouse. He told her and she was cool with it, so I guess just like motorcycles, it all depended on with whom I was riding.

Funtown closed in 1967 just about the time Six Flags opened. The remains took on a creepy life of their own. The Funtown sign remained up, rusting and decaying until the mid-Nineties when it was finally removed. Time and the elements reclaimed the remaining buildings and attractions. Kudzu eventually took over Humpty Dumpty sitting on the wall of the miniature golf course, along with the remains of a bear standing on his head, a one-eyed alien and a T-Rex towering over the vegetation.

But before Funtown and Six Flags was the granddaddy of them all, The Great Southeastern Fair. The Southeastern Fair was a yearly event at Lakewood Fairgrounds and was a huge deal in Atlanta. As kids we would anticipate the opening of the fair each year in October. The fair ran for two weeks and the midway consisted of rides, games of skill, burlesque shows, freak shows, carnival barkers, a Ferris wheel, a carousel and a veritable plethora of every type of unhealthy food imaginable. Livestock exhibitions and bake sales took place in the four large exhibition halls. There were the Wall Of Death motorcycle riders and the Hell Drivers auto daredevils at the Lakewood Speedway.

The Lakewood Speedway was built around a large lake at the back of the fairgrounds. The lake was once home to Atlanta's water works, which the city quickly outgrew. The one-mile racetrack was originally used for horse racing. Horse racing in Georgia? Horrors, say it's not so! It eventually became one of the premier tracks on the fledgling NASCAR racing circuit in the late Forties. Racing legend Richard Petty won his first race at Lakewood. His father, Lee Petty, finished second. Lee protested the race and demanded a recount of the laps. Upon recounting, it was determined that Lee was, in fact, the winner of the race and Richard was a lap down. When asked how could he do that to his own son, Lee replied, "When he wins, he's gonna win fair and square."

The first haunted house I ever went into was at The Southeastern Fair. I was seven years old and rode it with my father. That was also the night we went for a whirlybird ride and I got my wings as an Official Co-Pilot. The haunted house itself was on the main drag of the midway and you rode through it on train cars that seated two. You would go through the house, come out one of the windows and ride along the front facing the midway before disappearing back into the house through a window at the far end. I remember being scared out of my wits and having my head buried against my father most of the time. At one point we were riding through the house and a large arm that appeared to belong to a gorilla or some other type of simian ogre was protruding out of the wall. It was low enough to appear that it was going to swipe your head but just high enough to miss you entirely. I was sure it was going to get me, so I let out a shriek and hid my face in the safety of my father's chest again.

The signature ride on the midway was The Greyhound, a large wooden roller coaster named for its gray cars. It was big, it was noisy, it was fast and it was condemned at least two or three times before it was demolished in 1980 during the filming of *Smokey and the Bandit II*. I never rode The Greyhound. As a child I guess I was too young and by the last time I went to the fair in 1972 with a date, the old coaster was not running.

The Great Southeastern Fair ran for around sixty years, from 1916 until sometime in the mid-Seventies. The fairgrounds hosted a flea market once a month for about twenty years. The property has now been converted to sound stages and lots for television and movie production. A part of the old grandstand at the speedway is still miraculously standing, although like Funtown, kudzu and Mother Nature have devoured it.

I never thought that '92 would be my last trip to Six Flags. But it was and I can't really imagine going there now. My daughter bought season passes and went through her teenage years and into her twenties. I'm sure that my back and my ticker could handle the rides, but I'm not sure if my patience could endure the crowds. I know that my legs and my poor old feet could not take ten to twelve hours of walking on asphalt and concrete. But I must admit that I would love one more ride on The Great American Scream Machine in the front car. Up the lift, over the top and straight down the hill! The memories are there. They always will be.

Dodgeball

I played a lot of dodgeball growing up. We played it on the playground in grammar school. We played it in Boy Scout camp and FCA camp. And we played it in high school gym class. Dodgeball was a great game. Notice I said, "was." Dodgeball has been pretty much banned in all schools in the United States. It is referred to as a "human target game," and that's just not acceptable. Supposedly the game encourages bullying and infliction of pain. Whenever I played dodgeball in school, I always liked to be the one doing the dodging. To me that was a lot more fun and athletically demanding than throwing. Sure, a lot of our games in gym class were pretty intense, but that's what made them fun.

The truth of the matter is that most of the games we grew up playing are now banned. Some that have been eighty-sixed are unbelievable and defy good sense and logic, whatever little of that may be left in the world. The most mind-boggling is Tag. You can't run around, slap someone on the back and yell, "Tag, you're it!" anymore. Sometimes tags can turn into slapping, pushing or shoving and running can cause falls resulting in scrapes, cuts, bruises or other things we used to come in with from the playground and wore like badges of honor. I wonder if we are still allowed to play phone tag?

Remember Red Rover? We used to play that game on the playground with the whole class, not just boys against boys or girls against girls. The teacher would divide the class into two teams and we would line up holding hands and facing one another on the playground. One team would yell "Red rover, red rover, send So-and-So on over!" So-and-So would then run as fast as they could to some point in the chain and try to break through. If he or she broke through they could take the two players they broke through back to their team. If they failed to break through, they had to join the team that had called them over. The object of the game was to try and get all of the players on your team. Simple, playground fun, right? Well, we can't play it anymore because it's a contact game and contact games are dangerous and can cause injuries.

Touch football is out of the question. Kickball, one of the main games I remember playing at recess in grammar school, is virtually gone now because kids can sustain injuries from being hit with the ball. We used to have some righteous kickball games at Gresham Park Elementary. Again the teacher would divide the class into two co-ed teams. We would put down rubber bases, a rubber home plate and, with a red rubber ball, we had ourselves a kickball game. Kickball was played just like baseball, but the pitcher rolled the ball to the kicker standing at the plate. The kicker would then kick the ball into play and run to first base. The players in the field would catch the ball and throw it to the base, tag the runner with the ball or, if they were confident in their skills, throw the ball at the runner. If the runner was tagged or hit with the ball they were out. Kickball was a blast and we played it year round. There are kickball leagues everywhere now. But you can't play it in the schoolyard, because running isn't allowed, no tagging is allowed and certainly no throwing a ball at anyone is allowed.

We used to play a game in kindergarten called The Farmer In The Dell. I don't know if it has been banned, but it would not surprise me if schools refuse to play it now, because in the end one poor kid gets singled out as "the cheese." To play the game, everyone stands in a circle and one kid is designated as the farmer. Everyone sings "The farmer in the dell, the farmer in the dell; hi-ho the derry-oh, the farmer in the dell," while moving around in a circle. Then they go to the next verse, the farmer takes a wife, the farmer takes a wife, hi-ho the derry-oh the farmer takes a wife. The circle stops moving when the verse is over and the farmer chooses someone in the circle to be the wife. The wife joins him in the circle and the singing continues through the verses until there are only two left circling the ones in the middle. The final two verses are, "The rat takes the cheese, the rat takes the cheese, et cetera, et cetera, the rat takes the cheese." Then the farmer chooses one to be the rat and one player, the poor old cheese, is left standing all alone. Then, to add insult to injury, all the players in the middle sing, "The cheese stands alone, the cheese stands alone, et cetera, et cetera, the cheese stands alone." It is easy to see how this could traumatize a child, being picked on for being the cheese. But, in the next game the cheese gets to be the farmer. Therefore in the end everyone is subject to becoming the cheese and standing alone.

Musical chairs made the list, too. This one is particularly baffling. Apparently it has been blacklisted for a number of reasons, all of which seem ridiculous. It encourages exclusion, because if you don't sit on a chair fast enough, you're out. It encourages bullying and aggression because you're all fighting for a chair. And worst of all, it encourages competition because you're trying to win and beat everyone else to the last chair. As stated in an earlier chapter, Officer Don had the kids play Musical Chairs on *The Popeye Club.* I never saw any kids get ridiculed or start crying when they didn't get a chair and were out of the game. If any kid should have been upset it should have been the one who got the Ooey Gooey bag and the whole Clubhouse Gang laughed at them.

Competition, winning and losing are a part of life. Only one person gets the promotion or the scholarship, only one person wins the writing contest or the blue ribbon at the art show, only one person wins the last spot on the cheerleading squad. As Boomers we were taught this. In real life, everybody does not get a trophy.

If basically all games and recesses are banned, is the next step going to be doing away with academic competition as well? What about spelling bees? Won't kids be humiliated when they can't spell chrysanthemum and they're out of the game? Maybe I'm not the best person to be talking about spelling bees because I used to win them. Spelling was never a problem. But if Gresham Park Elementary or especially Walker had a math competition, I would have been out in the first round. I probably wouldn't have even made it to the first round. I wouldn't have made the B-Team or even the C-Team. I'm sure that it wouldn't have scarred me for life because I am well aware of my mathematical shortcomings. Lord knows I tried in class, but I believe math is something that you either get or you don't. I didn't get it. I was lost from the multiplication tables in the third grade through geometry in the tenth. Math landed me in summer school between sixth and seventh grade and eleventh and twelfth grade. I still struggled. So getting the boot from a mathematics competition wouldn't have bothered me in the least.

And finally, Pin The Tail On The Donkey is off the list as an acceptable activity at childrens' birthday parties. It seems that blindfolding a child, spinning them around and then having them walk with a sharp object has been deemed too dangerous.

Gym class is still taught in high schools. One year is generally required for graduation. I'm not in school and haven't been for a long time. Maybe it's better now, but I don't see how. Recess is being taken out of many elementary schools. And most of the kids whose schools still have recess can't play touch football, kickball, basketball, volleyball or Red Rover. There are no monkey bars and, worst of all, they can't play dodgeball. I wonder if they are still allowed to set up the gym for pep rallies or the lunchroom for dances? The memories are there. They always will be.

Volkswagens

I love Volkswagens. I have loved them for most of my life and certainly for all of my adolescent and adult life. I know all of the nicknames, Doodle Bug, Pregnant Roller Skate, German School Bus, Frog Car, Slug Bug, the list goes on. Nicknames aside, I find great beauty in the shape of the little car, the roundness, the lines and the contours. Most days, I find beauty in the simple yet brilliant engineering of the small air-cooled engine. Other days, not so much, but the good days far outweigh the bad days when I'm tempted to raise the deck lid and open fire with my riot gun.

I'm not sure exactly why I first became attracted to VW's, but I do remember it was around the time I was nine years old. I built a plastic model of a Bug, but something had sparked my interest in the little cars before then. The model was molded in black plastic and you had to glue the sides onto the body, which was unusual for most model cars. As I recall, I did a pretty good job of putting the kit together and displayed it proudly on my shelf with my other models of cars, airplanes, ships, boats and horror movie monsters.

My mother worked at Scripto in downtown Atlanta at the time. My father was a City of Atlanta fireman. It was summertime and the days he was on duty my schedule was to wake at eight, make my bed, eat my Frosted

Flakes and do my chores. Then I called him and he would come home, pick me up and take me back to the fire station. One morning I called him after completing my tasks and about fifteen minutes later I heard a beep-beep in the driveway. I looked out the living room window and there, below in the driveway, was my father climbing out of a little black Volkswagen. I remember running out the door yelling excitedly, “Daddy, Daddy, is it ours, is it ours?” He laughed and explained no, it belonged to one of the other firemen and he had let him borrow it to come and pick me up. The VW was black with red seats, just like my model sitting on the shelf. We rode up Rollingwood, turned left onto Flintwood, left onto Rockcliff and headed toward Fire Station Number 13 in East Atlanta. It was the first time I had ever ridden in a Bug, the first of untold thousands of times that would follow in the years and decades to come.

We finally got a VW in the fall of 1968. It was a 1956 model, dark green with white seats. My father bought it from the son of a fire department friend who lived on Parker Ranch Road. I would eventually become very good friends with his son and my buddy Moon would date his youngest daughter. The accessories were quite different on the Fifties models of the bugs than in later years. First of all there was no fuel gauge. You had to keep a log and figure mileage, or just remember the last time you put a couple of dollars worth of gas in the tank. If either one of those methods failed and you ran out, you would simply reach down and turn a small handle located under the dash at the front of the shifter tunnel. This opened the reserve tank and you could drive another forty miles or so. There was no radio and no heater. It had a small single back window. The larger back window would not be introduced until two years later. Our little Bug had turn signals, which were a factory-installed option and referred to as indicators in Europe. They weren't the flashing blinker type that are standard equipment and largely ignored today. They were semaphore indicators, which were located on the post between the front and back windows. When the indicator arm at the steering wheel was clicked to the left or the right it sent a signal to the appropriate semaphore arm. A small piston was activated, which flipped the signal up and out and a light on the signal began to blink. The piston then sent a signal back to the indicator light located in the speedometer, which blinked along with the light on the semaphore. When the indicator arm at the steering wheel was clicked off, it sent a signal to the piston, which turned off the flashing lights on the arm and speedometer, then pulled the semaphore back into place on the window post. Sometimes you really have to marvel at German engineering. Other times you look at something and ask, "What in the world were they thinking?"

We drove the Bug throughout the winter of '68. My father would take me to school in it and drive it to work.

That winter a snowstorm hit and cars could not make it up the steep hill on Rollingwood Lane. My father needed a pack of cigarettes, so he climbed in the Bug, puttered up the hill to Tenneco, puttered back home and lit up. Neither snow nor rain nor gloom of night keeps a man and his Bug from his pack of Lucky Strikes.

I learned to drive in the Bug. One Sunday afternoon when I was thirteen years old, Daddy took me out to the dirt road construction area at Clifton Springs Road and Panthersville Road where DeKalb College South Campus was being built. He put me behind the wheel of the little car and taught me to drive it in one afternoon. I've been a Bug Man ever since. At the end of the lesson he let me drive home. Times were a lot different back then.

Later on that spring we started disassembling the Bug to build a Meyers Manx fiberglass body dune buggy. That would be unthinkable today and by that time it had kind of become unthinkable to me. I had grown quite fond of the little green car and would have been perfectly content to have left it as it was. I even asked my father if we could keep it but was told no, we wanted to build a dune buggy. Years later, not long before Daddy passed away, I showed him a VW magazine I had bought which featured an article on a restored '56 Bug. It was dark green with white seats, just like ours. As we looked at the pictures I said to him, "You know, there's not a day goes by that I don't wish we had our '56 back." "Yeah," he said, "I know what you mean."

Allene is a Volkswagen Girl. It's one of the things that first attracted me to her, other than the fact that she is beautiful, smart, funny and talented. We are kindred spirits in many ways but first and foremost in all things Volkswagen. Up until we bought our Kia, she had never owned any type of vehicle other than a Volkswagen. She has an orange '72 Super Beetle, which she bought new. Now, that's a Bug Girl! Allene maintains that VW people are special people. "Gluttons for punishment," a friend used to say. The bond between lifelong VW people is undeniable. Allene's dad was a Bug Man, back when Bugs were all over the road. VW shops were everywhere and guys worked on them in their spare time out of carports, basements and garages, as was the case with Allene's dad. Her very first car was a gold 1958 Bug with a canvas sunroof. It was her sixteenth birthday present. She wanted a gunmetal gray Oldsmobile 442, but got the Bug instead. Her dad took black electrical tape and put the numbers "442" on each door. Being the good girl she is, Allene never complained.

Her VW quickly became one of the most popular and recognizable cars at Walker High School. It embodied everything that was fun about driving a Bug. It didn't have a back seat; you had to sit on milk crates. The key had been broken off in the ignition, so she had to stick a screwdriver in the switch and pull the choke handle while turning the screwdriver to crank it. If the engine wouldn't turn over, she jiggled the cables on the battery. She learned all the tricks and shortcuts that VW people eventually learned. The sound system was a portable Magnavox radio wedged in between the open glove compartment door and the Holy [Crap] Bar. The Holy [Crap] Bar was the handle on the dashboard of the earlier Bugs. It was moved to above the passenger door in '73. Originally intended to aid in getting out of the vehicle, the true purpose of the bar was, in a moment of motoring crisis, the passenger grabbed onto it and yelled "HOLY [CRAP]!

Allene taught several friends to drive in the old gold ragtop and they all wound up owning VWs themselves. Allene got a '67 model when she went away to college at Georgia Southern. She never knew what had happened to the little gold '58 until years later. Raleigh, a lifelong family friend who worked with Allene's dad in his garage, bought it after Allene went away to college at Georgia Southern. He sold the car to a friend of his, who wrecked it and sold it for parts. That's the type of thing you wish you never knew.

There was a veritable plethora of Bugs at Walker High School, driven by students and teachers alike. A guy named Big E had a beige mid-Sixties model Bug. He put a Hurst T-handle knob on the gear shifter, had the tires mounted on Cragar mag wheels and put *Hurst VW* in silver stick-on letters on the front quarter panels. Allene's friend Boat had a beautiful orange Karmann Ghia convertible until one day a German Shepherd ran out in front of her. That was the end of the German Shepherd and the Karmann Ghia.

Allene's sister drove a '66 Bug in high school, too. The windshield wipers quit working, which is not an odd occurrence on a '66 Bug. She tied a shoestring around the arm of the passenger-side wiper, ran it around the windshield post, through the vent window and attached it to the Holy [Crap] Bar. Whenever it started to rain, she would unhook the shoestring from the Holy [Crap] Bar, pull and let go in a gentle rhythm, clearing her windshield of the falling rain. Oh, the ingenuity of Volkswagen people. Her Daddy was quite proud of her.

My buddy Moon had a yellow '71 Karmann Ghia that should have been bronzed before he sold it. If ever there was a testament to the durability and the toughness of a Volkswagen, it was Moon's Karmann Ghia. I have never seen a car abused like that one and still crank and go every time he climbed in. He would fly down dirt roads fishtailing and aiming for potholes. He cut doughnuts in it, painfully and incorrectly downshifted through curves and, to my knowledge, never had the oil changed or the valves adjusted in the four years he owned the car. It is a miracle that the engine never blew up. He bought a black Chevy Laguna in ’74 and I don’t know what happened to the Karmann Ghia. All I know is that it ought to be in a museum somewhere in Wolfsburg.

I bought a Bug my junior year at Walker. It was a pale green ’63 model and remains the best bargain I have ever had in a car. I bought it off of a buddy for seventy-five dollars. I tinkered with it, drove it to school a couple of days a week and even went out on a few dates in it. Then I let my father talk me into using it to build another dune buggy. I resisted at first, but he kept at me and I eventually caved in. He built a beautiful metalflake blue street buggy and then wouldn’t let me drive it. When I did, the car went through a fifty-six-point inspection when I got home. The final straw was the day Moon and I took it for a Sunday drive and drove the car down a few dirt roads. I didn’t fishtail it or aim for potholes, but I did bring it home with a little bit of mud on the tires. My old man went ballistic. He was convinced that Moon and I had taken it out trail riding and railed accusatory profanities at me. That was the last time I drove it. It sat parked in the carport in Rex for about six or eight months until it was finally sold.

When I was seventeen I bought a ‘69 Mach 1 Mustang. It was black with a red interior, slotted disc wheels and was absolutely beautiful. I drove it, loved it and cared for it until I sold it during the so-called gas shortage of the mid-Seventies. I kick myself daily now for doing so.

I bought a yellow '73 Super Beetle, which was a great little car and I drove it for fifteen years. But every time I'm watching one of those auto auction shows and they roll out a '69 Mach 1, my stomach knots up and turns when I see what it sells for.

I had always wanted a VW convertible. In the summer of '83 I sold my Ford Ranger 150 pickup and bought a '69 convertible from a friend for five hundred dollars and a canoe. The car was pale yellow and the back floor pan was rusted out. At one point in time it had a white top, but all that was left was the frame and a few strips of tattered cloth. I didn't care. The car was, like all Volkswagens, an absolute blast to drive. There was a canvas cover for the top when it was folded down, so I covered the frames with that and drove it the rest of the summer with no top.

I began disassembling the car in the fall and began the restoration work. I painted the car red, had a black top put on it and drove it for five years before turning it over one winter to a friend who owned a body shop. He stripped the paint off, put in new floor pans, painted the car light beige, replaced all the chrome trim and both outside rear-view mirrors. The car looked brand new. I drove it for years, sometimes as a commuter car before storing it in a family member's basement. We were at his house recently and I went down to visit with my little buddy. I sat with him, talked to him and told him that I missed him. I promised to get off my duff, tune him up and take him for a spin.

I stared at the little car for a long time. The memories are there. They always will be.

Putt-Putt and Idlewood

I grew up playing miniature golf. Miniature golf is often referred to as Putt-Putt or Goofy Golf. Putt-Putt is a franchise name and Goofy Golf is a family-owned business in Destin and Fort Walton Beach, Florida. As a kid growing up, mini-golf was great for several reasons. First and foremost, you could play on your allowance and grass-cutting budget. You didn't have to buy a set of clubs because the putters and multi-colored balls were supplied at the counter. You could walk or ride your bike to the course. A typical round lasted less than an hour. You didn't have to become proficient at the full golf swing, only the putting stroke. And best of all, you could play by yourself or with a friend or three, because nobody frowned on kids playing. There weren't any old geezers sitting on a bench by the first tee, lighting their Chesterfields, clicking their Zippos, exhaling blue smoke, looking at you with total disdain and grumbling about [darn] kids.

The first place I remember playing miniature golf was in Longview, Texas. My aunt, uncle and cousin lived in Longview, which is located about one hundred and twenty-five miles east of Dallas. On our summer trips to Dallas we would stop in Longview for the night, then we would all continue on to Dallas the next morning. My uncle was a golfer and was the first in the family to hit a hole-in-one. My father made him a ceramic ashtray with a big gold number one with a hole in it. Every time we went to Longview I would ask my uncle if we could play "putt-putt." He was a good man and never said no. After dinner he, my father, my cousin and I would go out to the mini-golf course.

The name of the Longview mini-golf course escapes me, but the thing I remember distinctly about it was that the surface of the holes was sawdust dyed green. This meant a lot of footprints on the putting surface, so workers were constantly walking the course and smoothing the sawdust by dragging pieces of carpet attached to ropes tied around their waists. I was probably only six or seven the first time we played there and I was hooked. We always played at night, under the lights. I don't remember ever playing during the day, but the memories of the evenings playing mini-golf in Longview are some of the fondest of my childhood.

My cousin would come to visit us in Atlanta periodically and he would take me to play the miniature courses at Glenwood Hills and Misty Waters. There was a miniature course at Clifton Springs too. I don't remember playing it, probably because I was more concerned with hitting the beach and the water.

I tried to set up a mini-golf course in our back yard. I was going to charge a quarter a round and get rich. I drew up plans and mapped out the holes. The course started at the top of the yard on the flat part next to my father's grill that he made from a fifty-five-gallon drum. The idea was to putt over the brick retaining wall and off of the patio to the green below. You then proceeded to follow the holes down to the bottom of the yard and then back up to the patio. I spray painted a piece of plywood green and set up a ramp from the yard back onto the patio. You putted up the ramp to the eighteenth green on the patio. If you made a hole-in-one, you got a free round. The only problem was that the grass in our back yard, while lush, was not very conducive to putting. My father flipped out when I mowed the grass tight for the fairways and my mother had a cow when I started digging holes in the yard and burying tin cans for the cups. So that was the end of the Rollingwood Backyard Mini-Golf venture.

A Putt-Putt course opened up in Gresham Park in the early Seventies. I began to play there a lot, meeting friends and spending an afternoon or an evening trying to put the orange, yellow or green ball into the hole. Putt-Putt was different than a lot of miniature golf courses inasmuch as it required a bit more skill, similar to the course in Longview. There were two eighteen-hole courses at the Gresham Park Putt-Putt. Par on all of the holes was two. On some of them, par was next to impossible. Only the best putters were able to score a two. The last hole on one of the courses was a steep slope up to the cup. On the last hole of the other course, you hit the ball into a metal semicircle drum, which would feed the ball toward the cup, which was on a platform just ahead of the tee. If you scored a hole-in-one on either of these holes, you won a free game. I became quite proficient at scoring a hole-in-one on the semicircle drum hole. The trick was to hit a particular spot on the drum at the right speed and the ball would go up the drum, onto the green, bounce off the back wall and feed directly into the cup.

My friend Kyle and I began to play Putt-Putt on a regular basis. Kyle was my football buddy. He played fullback, I played center. Kyle was also a very good golfer. He was already shooting in the seventies at age fifteen. After the first game of the season in the tenth grade he quit football to play golf. We all thought he was crazy. He became a star high school golfer and received a golf scholarship to Wake Forest University. So Kyle wasn't crazy after all. Once we were on the far end of the Putt-Putt course and Kyle yelled "ORR ON THE SLAP SHOT!" and took a full swing with the putter at the orange ball resting on the little rubber mat tee. The ball took off like a rocket shot, easily cleared the concrete block wall of the course and landed somewhere in the neighborhood that backed up to the course. We didn't hear any glass break or anyone scream, so everything must have been okay. Kyle was a very good golfer.

There was also a Putt-Putt course in Forest Park. This

was one of the most popular Putt-Putt courses in the Atlanta area and certainly one of the tops in terms of longevity. Located on Jonesboro Road next to Shoney's, it opened about the same time as the Putt-Putt in Gresham Park and finally closed sometime in the Nineties. Shoney's was the Forest Park cruising spot. Souped-up cars would circle the building and be parked in the drive-in spaces constantly and Putt-Putt was always busy.

I took my daughter there to play one evening when she was about six or seven years old. It seemed like a good age to introduce her to Putt-Putt. One of the holes had two wooden blocks jutting out from each side, making a narrow opening in the middle. The back of the hole had a rise to it and the cup was cut in the far-right corner. My daughter stepped up to the tee and hit her shot. The ball went through the opening, up the rise and curved into the cup. She started screaming and jumping up and down. I high fived and hugged her, then went to the counter and got another ball. I put her hole-in-one ball in my pocket and took her to Shoney's afterward for a milk shake. I didn't tell her about the tradition that if you hit a hole-in-one, the drinks are on you. The orange ball sat on her shelf along with her softball trophies for years. I have no clue what happened to it, but I sure would like to have it in my souvenir ball rack now.

When Mary Jane and I got married, we went to Destin,

Florida on our honeymoon. This was a time when there was very little in Destin, just a few hotels and miles upon miles of white sand and Florida underbrush. We had to go into Fort Walton in the evenings for dinner because there were virtually no restaurants in Destin. Across the street from our hotel was a miniature golf course called Magic Carpet Golf. We played there every night because there was nothing else to do. It was classic Florida mini-golf with windmills, loop-the-loops and a hole where you hit the ball into an alligator's mouth and it came out the other end. We managed to get a couple of holes-in-one the first night and won a couple of free games. We went back the next night and every night for the remainder of the week. It was a harbinger of things to come.

I got a set of golf clubs when I was fifteen. They were Spalding Par Plays from Woolworth's at South DeKalb Mall. I played a couple of times at Clifton Springs, stuck them in my closet and didn't pick them up again for twelve years. Mary Jane's dad played golf and often talked about the game. That kind of piqued my interest, coupled with the fact that a lot of baseball and football players were golfers, so maybe it wasn't such a wimpy game after all. In the summer of '81 something happened that had a profound influence on us. We saw the movie *Caddyshack.* We laughed hysterically at the antics of Al Czervik, Carl Spagler, Ty Webb, Judge Smails, Danny Noonan and Lacey Underall at Bushwood

Country Club. Afterwards I said to Mary Jane, "You know, maybe we ought to try playing golf." I pulled my old golf bag out of the closet at my parents' house, dusted off the clubs and we began hitting shots with plastic practice balls in our back yard.

One evening we had Mary Jane's friend Heidi down for a barbecue. Standing around the grill, her husband Tom and I got into a discussion about golf. He said he played the game and I told him that we had been practicing but had not played yet. We decided that we would all get together the following day and play a round. Mary Jane had never played and I had only played the few times at Clifton Springs. That was all about to change. "Where are we going to play?" they all asked. "There's a course over on Highway 212 called Idlewood," I said. "We'll play there."

Idlewood Golf Course was a family-owned course built on farmland in 1963. It was way out in the country back then and was still fairly rural at the time we started playing there. It was a nine-hole layout with the first four holes circling the perimeter of the property. The remainder of the holes ran parallel in the middle, with the exception of the ninth hole which was a par three that ran along the top of the course with the green adjacent to the one-story, cinder block clubhouse. The holes were all straight, no doglegs and the four in the middle were like a war zone. You needed a football helmet for protection from errant shots that were always flying from the tees into the adjacent fairways. There were no sand traps and no hills to speak of, although the land sloped down from the highway to Pole Bridge Creek at the bottom of the property. There was one stand of trees and two small ponds on the course. The stand of trees stood between the second and eighth fairway. One of the ponds was in front of the seventh tee, the other in front of the eighth green. There was only one set of tees and the longest hole on the course was the lone par five. It measured four hundred and eighty-five yards and ran along the eastern border of the property.

The first day we played it was obvious that we had no clue what we were doing. Tom had claimed that he played golf. If so, it couldn't have been very often. He wasn't very athletic anyway and hacked it around just like the rest of us. I swung and missed three times on the first tee. When I finally made contact I hit a ground ball about fifty yards down the fairway. But it was in the middle and that was all that mattered. A few holes later I was standing behind Heidi and to her left. Somehow she hit the ball backwards and it almost took my head off. On the next tee I chopped under the ball with the driver and the ball flew up and hit me in the left eye, rendering me temporarily blind with my wife and friends rolling on the ground, convulsing with laughter. The whole scene looked like a blooper reel out of a Three Stooges short.

Mary Jane and I began to play golf more and more, eventually once a week. And we always played at Idlewood. It was inexpensive, fun and there were a lot of characters that hung out there, mostly older retirees. We really came to love and appreciate the course itself. It is where we learned to play the game and we always referred to it as "our Saint Andrews."

We used to have feral cats that would show up at our house when our female cat would go into heat. Mary Jane would get traps from Animal Control, catch one and then have me drive the prisoner to Idlewood and release him. There were woods all around and a neighborhood adjacent to the first fairway. That way, she figured, the cat would have a chance and it was better than having the authorities come and pick the animal up. This had to be done extremely early on a Saturday morning, because old guys would start showing up around seven in the morning to sit around and drink coffee. So, in the pre-dawn hours I would rise, load the trap in the back of my El Camino, drive to Idlewood, back the tailgate up to the woods at the top of the parking lot and open up the trap. I never had a cat that was hesitant about jumping out of the trap and running into the woods.

There was one cat in particular who would not go away. He was black with half of his tail and one ear missing. We called him Bob because of his tail. Bob was also ornery, mean and very smart because we couldn't trap him. He could eat all the food without stepping on the release and closing the trap. One day Bob became careless and got caught in the trap. The next morning I loaded him in the El Camino and took him to the golf course. As he ran out of the cage he stopped at the edge of the tailgate, hissed a profanity at me, jumped down and ran into the woods. Mary Jane and I played golf the next weekend and I went to pay our green fee while she loaded the bags onto the cart. When I got to the clubhouse, sitting at the door beside a food and water bowl was Bob. He hissed at me and I went inside. "When did y'all get the cat?" I asked Mac, who worked behind the counter. "Oh, he showed up about a week ago," said Mac. "He won't leave." "What's his name?" I asked. "Bob," he said. "We named him that because of his tail." I walked back outside and looked at Bob. He looked back and we both stared at each other for a few seconds. He knew and I knew. "You ought to thank me, you know," I said. He hissed at me again. I walked to our golf cart where Mary Jane was finishing loading the bags. "You're not going to believe who's sitting outside of the clubhouse," I said to her. "Who?" she asked.

"Bob."

"Bob who?"

"Bob the cat."

"Bob, our cat?"

"Yep. Apparently he lives here now."

"Are you serious?"
"You'll see for yourself in just a minute."
"Wow."
"It gets even better. You're not going to believe what they named him."
"Bob, because of his tail."
"How did you know that?"
"Well, it's a pretty obvious name."
Bob slowly came to terms with us. He eventually let Mary Jane pet him. I was never brave enough to try.

Idlewood closed in the late Nineties. On a spring Saturday morning we loaded up the clubs and headed that way. There was a chain across the gravel entrance to the parking lot. We came back the next day after church. The chain was still there and the parking lot was empty. I called the course the next morning from work and the number had been disconnected. I called Mary Jane and I thought she was going to start crying. "I wonder what happened to poor Bob?" she said. "Go by there this afternoon and see if you can find him." I explained to her that would be trespassing and even if I found Bob, he hated me and would probably shred my arms if I tried to pick him up.

A subdivision was built on the property, about two hundred houses shoehorned into ten acres. I drove through it once in our VW convertible, which was the car that we usually took to the golf course. It was very strange driving on the property, down the first fairway, over the second hole that was the first par three and turning left at the third tee. The stand of trees was gone, along with both of the ponds. The houses were cracker boxes, stacked right next to one another with no yards to speak of. I circled the subdivision and stopped at the top of the hill on the old par-five fourth hole. I tried to look out and envision the old course but couldn't because I was looking right into someone's garage. It was heartbreaking. I slowly circled around to the front of the subdivision and past where the old cinder block clubhouse sat. I didn't see Bob anywhere. I took a right and pulled out of the subdivision, turned left onto Highway 212 and headed toward home. I never rode through Idlewood again. The memories are there. They always will be.

Friday Night Lights

I played football all five years I attended Walker High School and those were some of the greatest years of my life. We endured some tough seasons and didn't win a lot of games, but we were teammates, brothers-in-arms and friends. Wrestling was the number one sport at Walker, but football ran a close second. We worked hard and gave it all we had in practice and on game nights. And game nights were, for the most part, at Panthersville Stadium.

Built in 1968, Panthersville Stadium was originally shared by five area schools, Walker, Southwest DeKalb, Columbia, Gordon and Lithonia. On Friday nights for so very many of us, Panthersville was the center of the universe. The stadium was dedicated on September 27, 1968. Walker vs. Southwest DeKalb was the first game played there, with SWD winning 35-26. I played in Panthersville's second game, which was the very next morning. Walker and SWD's eighth-grade teams kicked off at 8 a.m. I don't remember the score, but we won.

For a kid who had only played football for two years in the intramural league at Gresham Park and the rest of his games on the flood plain in Bubba-Bubba's side yard, playing at Panthersville was like playing in Atlanta Stadium. We rode a bus to the game. The stadium had real locker rooms. We had official referees, cheerleaders, a manager and a statistician. This was the big time. There were mostly parents, grandparents and a few kids from school in the seats for those eighth-grade games, but that was okay. You were playing for Walker High School and that was all that mattered.

On Friday nights, pretty much every student, parent and teacher was in the stadium, on the sidelines or on the field. The cross country team ran meets before the football games, four laps around the track. The cheerleaders cheered, the bands marched and played, the drill teams performed with precision and the majorettes twirled fire batons. We crowned homecoming queens, sometimes in the driving rain. We performed and played in both the stifling heat and the freezing cold. We persevered and the elements never took away from the splendor and the pageantry.

To get in shape for the upcoming two-a-day summer practices, we would go to Panthersville and run the steps. The stadium was pretty much left open all the time back then and we would sometimes play pick up games there on Sundays. My father, my friend Billy and I used to shoot model rockets off of the gravel parking lot behind the stadium. Sometimes a rocket would float back to earth on its parachute and land in the middle of the field. Billy and I would jump the fence and go retrieve it. No one cared and no one called the cops.

The first game of my tenth-grade season, we played

Southwest DeKalb in a B-Team night game. It was the first game I had ever started. I weighed in at a hundred and forty pounds and played center. While we were warming up I saw an ambulance coming down Clifton Springs Road, followed by a fire truck. They both turned into the stadium. I didn't think twice about it. There was more important business at hand.

At halftime one of the managers told me that someone wanted to see me at the door. I went to the door and it was a kid who had lived up the street from us in Gresham Park. He had moved to Southwest DeKalb a few years earlier. His parents and my parents were good friends. He had a strange look on his face and told me, "I just wanted you to know that your father had a heart attack before the game started. Horis Ward came and got him." Horis Ward owned a funeral home on Candler Road. This was in the days before EMTs so it was not uncommon for funeral homes to operate an ambulance service as well. As it turned out, they had taken him to Crawford Long Hospital, but I didn't know that. For all I knew, he was at the funeral home up on Candler Road. Five minutes later I was standing on the forty-yard line getting ready for us to kick off. I was numb, shocked and frightened, but as soon as the whistle blew and the ball boomed into the night sky, I tore off down the field screaming like a banshee. I took out three guys and hit the ball carrier at the twenty-five yard line. He went one way and the ball went the other. They got the ball back, but we went on to win. My father recovered, but he did not get out of the hospital in time to see any of our games except for the last one of the season. We played Lithonia and won, on a gray and damp November morning.

Memorial Stadium, which was located on the campus of DeKalb Community College in Clarkston, opened about the same time as Panthersville. We played our second game of the season in the eighth grade there. Towers, Clarkston and Stone Mountain shared the stadium. It was double sided and seated about ten thousand people. There was hardly a fraction of that number attending the game that morning, but after playing our first game in Panthersville, running on the field and looking up at the tall concrete stands was like running onto the field at Sanford Stadium in Athens.

We played Clarkston in Memorial Stadium the third game of the season my senior year. My friend Freddie was a junior, played fullback and was running through the Clarkston defense like they were tackling dummies the whole first quarter. On the first play of the second quarter, Freddie took a lick to the head and it knocked him into the following Tuesday. That turned things around. Clarkston took over the game and won. This was at a time when head injuries were not given the proper attention and due diligence that they are today. The general diagnosis back then was if you knew your name, you were good to go back in. Freddie didn't know his name and he didn't go back in. He wasn't even sure what planet he was on. He sat on the bench, staring into space with his mouth open. I trotted off the field after one of the numerous times Clarkston kicked off to us and sat next to him on the fence. Freddie looked at me with a look of utter confusion on his face. "Who are you?" he asked.

"I'm your buddy Jimmy."

"Where are we?"

"We're at Memorial Stadium."

"How did we get here?"

"We rode here in the bus."

"We rode in a bus?"

"Yep."

"What are we doing here?"

"We're playing football. You were carrying the ball great in the first quarter."

"I carried the ball?"

"Yeah, you were running great, Freddie."

"Who?'

Clarkston was already up by a lopsided score when we went into the locker room at halftime. Coach H. came storming through the door, chewing nails and spitting vinegar. Coach H. had a thyroid problem, so his eyes kind of bugged out under normal circumstances. They looked like ping-pong balls about to pop out of their sockets when he hit the door. He grabbed a chair, slung it against the lockers and began screaming and cursing. Freddie jumped about three feet backwards with a look of sheer terror on his face that read, “Who is this man and why is he screaming so much?” Coach H.’s locker room tirade didn’t do any good and Clarkston beat us by at least a couple of touchdowns. Freddie lived in the same neighborhood as my buddy Moon, so the next day I drove over to Moon’s and we went to see Freddie. Freddie answered the door and had recovered his senses and faculties. “Man, I’ve got a splitting headache,” he said. “Did we lose?” “Yeah, pretty bad,” said Moon. “If you wouldn’t have been knocked out of the game it would have been a different story,” I said. “Do you remember any of it?” “No,” he said, “the last thing I remember is getting on the bus when we were leaving the school.”

The last game of that season was the last organized football game I would ever play. We were ready to take the field against Avondale at Panthersville. The seniors were all honorary captains. We were to lead the team on the field and participate in the coin toss. As we were leaving the locker room, screaming, hollering, fired up and and ready to play, I ran out and saw my father standing in front of the door. He grabbed my arm and pulled me to one side. He had hired Mr. Earl, our chemistry teacher and school photographer, to take my picture. I had to stand there while Mr. Earl adjusted the settings on his camera and my teammates ran past me.

I was bouncing up and down, rocking back and forth and ready to go. Mr. Earl raised his camera and my father said, "Smile, Jimmy." I didn't smile and as soon as Mr. Earl snapped the picture I was gone. I ran down the stairs as fast as I could in my cleats. The seniors were already huddling with the officials at midfield. I ran straight toward them, feeling as if every eye in the stadium was on me.

A friend of mine played at Stockbridge High in the mid-Eighties. They would travel to Panthersville to play Walker, who was in their region at the time. Stockbridge was still playing in the old stadium behind the school on North Henry Boulevard. My friend said that compared to that, playing in Panthersville was like playing in Texas Stadium.

Of all the stadiums in DeKalb County and beyond, none struck fear in your heart like Death Valley. Death Valley was Avondale High School's stadium. It was named as such because it was located in a valley behind the school and because of what usually happened to those who had the misfortune to venture in there. Avondale was a perennial football powerhouse in the Sixties and early Seventies, winning a slew of regional championships and three state championships. Any time you walked into that stadium you were pretty much assured that you were going to get a butt-whoopin'. The Blue Devils practiced at the stadium as well, so that meant by the third or fourth game most of the grass was gone and the field was a combination of dirt and rocks. The first time I ever played there was in my eighth-grade year. It was a perfect fall day, halfway through the season and we got our jocks handed to us, 44-0. It was the only game we lost that year. In my five years at Walker, we never beat Avondale. The closest we came was the last game of my senior season, when they beat us 21-7.

After fifty-seven years, Avondale High closed its doors as a public school in 2011. It is now a magnet school for the arts, so the school was not leveled. The stadium is still in use. About a year before the school closed, I delivered a piece of artwork to a friend who lived on Clarendon Avenue. On the way to her house, I passed the school and decided on a whim to turn down Berkeley Road, which runs adjacent to the north end of the stadium. I drove down the street, turned around at Dunwick Drive, drove slowly back up Berkeley and stopped about halfway up the hill. I sat and stared at the stadium for a long time. It appeared to be in good shape, but it looked so small. And from the vantage point of decades removed, it certainly did not look intimidating. In research, I came across a review that described the stadium as "quaint." I have been suited up on that field and it was anything but "quaint." Unless you were a Blue Devil, Death Valley was no place for the faint of heart on a Friday night. The memories are there. They always will be.

Eagles, Generals, Panthers, Titans and Saints

Growing up in our time and season, most of the schools were in close proximity to one another. Many of us had a lot of friends that lived in different school districts and as a result we all went to different schools together. The rivalries that sprung up between those schools were the natural result of geography and the fact that a lot us had known one another since childhood.

A lot of those friendships were formed through sports, be it baseball, softball, football, cheerleading or the DeKalb All-Stars Drill Team. Kids from different areas came to the different rec centers and parks to play, either in the organized leagues or weekend pickup games. A friend I used to work with grew up in East Point, went to Headland High School and played baseball at DeKalb Memorial Park on Glenwood Road.

A lot of kids from Gordon played ball at Gresham Park because that was the park that was closest to their neighborhoods. Around the Flat Shoals, Clifton Springs and Whites Mill areas, the dividing lines between Walker and Gordon were bizarre, to say the least. The side of Flat Shoals Road that was closer to Walker was in the Gordon district. The opposite side, which was closer to Gordon, was in the Walker District. A subdivision between Flat Shoals Road and Clifton Springs Road was in the Walker district, but the subdivision right next to it was in the Gordon district.

That would have seemed to make Walker and Gordon instant rivals, but that was not necessarily the case. There was a rivalry between the Generals and the Warhawks, to be sure, but it was more like a friendly rivalry. The football games were more like two brothers being in a fight.

That was not the case with Walker and Columbia High School. The two were archrivals, not only in sports but also in civic clubs, academics and social life. Columbia's team name was the Eagles. Their colors were blue and orange. The week leading up to one of the football games a group of sports enthusiasts from Walker went over to Columbia one night, ran a rubber chicken up the flag pole and painted the mailbox crimson and silver. In retaliation, a group of sports enthusiasts from Columbia came to Walker the following night, ran the same rubber chicken up the flagpole and painted our mailbox blue and orange. Not to be outdone, the group of sports enthusiasts from Walker staked out the buses carrying the team, the band, the majorettes, the drill team and the cheerleaders to Panthersville Stadium on game night. While the buses were enroute on I-20, several carloads of enthusiasts pulled up next to the bus carrying the cheerleaders and mooned them. I'm not sure if that one was ever topped. My senior year we won exactly one game, a 14-12 victory over Columbia. That made the season. There is a picture in the yearbook of the poor old rubber chicken putting his foot in his mouth.

Walker was a perennial champion in wrestling, winning five state championships in a row. Columbia had a very strong wrestling program as well, but could never quite beat Walker in the regular season matches or the county, region or state tournaments. I think that was the main reason behind the intense rivalry between the two schools. When Walker's run of championships ended in 1972, the team that won the state championship was Columbia.

The rivalry extended beyond the athletic fields. I belonged to Jr. Civitan and the club that we were always in direct competition with was Columbia. Every spring there would be a statewide convention at Jekyll Island. It was a long weekend of fun and festivities. There were meetings in the mornings and the evenings, followed each night by a dance with a live band. There was a beauty pageant, speeches and award ceremonies. The convention was topped off on Saturday evening with the announcement of the winner of the Hastings Award, which was given to the top club in the state. My junior year Columbia won Hastings. My senior year we won. Not everyone got a trophy when it came to Jr. Civitan and the Hastings Award.

A lot of Walker students moved to the Southwest DeKalb

area in the early Seventies, so many of us knew one another. Similar to Gordon, there was not much of a rivalry between the Panthers and us. Their main rival was Avondale. Everybody wanted to beat Avondale and Southwest DeKalb because they were two of the best football programs in the state. That made for a natural rivalry between the two schools. Avondale won three state championships and Southwest DeKalb won the state title our senior season.

In the fall and winter of 1973 I worked in the warehouse at Sears on Ponce De Leon Avenue while attending DeKalb Community College. One of the guys I worked with was a senior at Southwest DeKalb and we became good friends. I would ride over to the school after classes at DeKalb to see him and sometimes we would ride in to work together.

One afternoon I rode over and ran into an old friend I had known since kindergarten named Parker. Parker had a black, souped-up 1969 Dodge Charger with a 383 hemi engine, mag wheels and custom white panel stripes on the side. We took it for a ride up Rainbow Drive, down Flat Shoals Road and turned back up Boring Road toward the school. About halfway up Boring Road we met a DeKalb County police car coming in the opposite direction. "He's going to follow us," said Parker. "They follow me all the time in this car." I turned around to look and sure enough the gold Plymouth Fury had pulled into a driveway and was turning around. “Yep, he’s turning around,” I said. “Here he comes.”

We pulled up to the intersection where Boring Road meets Kelly Chapel Road. “Which way should I go?” asked Parker. “Take a left and go back to the school,” I said. I figured if we could make it back to the parking lot we would be okay. Just then there was a loud crash and the car lurched forward. We both turned around and looked. The police car had rear-ended us and the nose of the gold Fury was plowed into the rear bumper of the Charger. The officer jumped out of the car and was frantically waving his arms, jumping up and down and running around in circles. He said that was the third accident he had been involved in in the last six months that was his fault. I started to suggest he look for a different line of work but thought better of it. Apparently he had forgotten all about whatever the reason was that he was following us. The officer wrote himself a ticket and while he was writing I looked at Parker and said, “I’m going to walk back to the school. I’ve got to go to work.” I split and the officer never paid me a lick of attention. He obviously had other things on his mind at that particular moment.

About a week or so later I bumped into Parker again. He said that the wreck had only bent the plastic panel beneath the bumper. Per the county’s instructions he had taken the car for an insurance appraisal. The claims adjuster inspected the damage, filled out the paperwork and cut Parker a check for three hundred dollars. Parker walked out of the appraisal office, pulled the plastic panel back into place and drove away. He said that he was going to use the money to go to Daytona at spring break. That was when you could go to Daytona for a week at spring break on three hundred dollars. We never knew what happened to the officer that was driving, but my guess is that he didn't remain in law enforcement much longer.

Towers was another school that Walker squared off against yearly in all sports, but we never really had much of a rivalry. The Titans used to host a basketball tournament each year over the holidays called the Towers Christmas Tournament. Walker usually got bounced pretty early, but it was a lot of fun to attend because you always saw a lot of people that you knew.

A friend of mine who went to Clarkston High said that Clarkston hated Avondale until the new Stone Mountain High was built and then those two schools became instant rivals.

In the fall of 1972 Cedar Grove High School opened. That meant that all tenth graders and under from Walker and Southwest DeKalb who lived within the newly defined district went to Cedar Grove. Their team name was the Saints and their colors were light blue and dark blue. Most of us at Walker knew most of the entire student body at Cedar Grove and vice versa. But since the highest grade in Cedar Grove was the tenth grade, we did not play them in any sport so there really wasn't a rivalry there at all. They didn't field a varsity team until 1974 and didn't play Walker until the 1976 season, so if a rivalry developed it was later.

Cedar Grove's first graduating class was 1975. They now have a reunion once every five years for the classes of '75 through '80, due to the fact that it was such a small school with small graduating classes. My friend Beera is on the committee for each reunion and he always tries to get me to attend. "You know most everybody there and they all know you," he told me. He's right. Maybe I'll go one year. He's convinced I would have a great time and fit right in. I'm sure that I would, if they wouldn't mind an old Warhawk in the middle of a bunch of Saints. The memories are there. They always will be.

Tails, A Top Hat and Hot Pants

The focal of school social life were the dances. There were dances on Saturday nights in the gym every few weeks, the first usually being the weekend of the first week of school. The dances featured a lot of local bands, some of which would go on to become quite well known. Most of the others faded into obscurity. The cost to get in was usually fifty cents for stag and seventy-five cents for drag, terms that probably could not be used today. Thin rubber mats covered the hardwood floor of the gymnasium and the band played on the stage. The bleachers were pulled out on either side and kids sat on each side in groups, couples or alone. Sometimes it would take half a night to work up the nerve to ask someone special to dance. After all, dancing was everything and holding hands meant something, as is quoted in the song.

At Walker, a faculty member or administrator came up with the brilliant idea of having dances in the morning before school. The dances lasted for about an hour, from seven in the morning until eight, giving students enough time to rock out and still make it to homeroom on time. I remember going down to the locker room to drop my laundered football gear in my locker, walking past the gym and taking a look inside. The lights were down, the music was blasting and the floor was full of revelers, spinning and dancing to questionable covers of Cream,

Steppenwolf and Deep Purple. The bands were generally neighborhood garage bands comprised of students. All that changed one morning when a friend, who shall remain anonymous, was onstage with his band. He suddenly had a Pete Townshend moment and grabbed his bass guitar by the tuning head and began swinging it like a pickaxe, smashing the body on the stage floor. The lights came up immediately and that was the end of that and all subsequent morning dances. It was the talk of the school all day and my friend became a pariah in the local garage band scene for denying all of the budding local musicians a venue to showcase their talents.

The weekly dances were a blast, but could not compare to the semi-formal dances held three times each year. They were the Homecoming Dance in the fall, the Holly Ball at Christmas and the Sweetheart Dance in February. These dances were not held in the gym, but in the cozier and more intimate atmosphere of the school lunchroom. I don't mean this facetiously. The lunchroom was transformed into a ballroom, with tables for couples on each side and a dance floor in front of the stage. The Homecoming Dance was the first big dance of the school year. It took place at the school on the Saturday night following the Homecoming game on Friday night. It was semi-formal, which meant that the boys wore jackets and ties and the girls wore mid-length to long dresses. Each couple had their picture made together and there was a theme for each year. The first one that I went to was in my tenth-grade year. I do not remember the theme from that year, but my junior year was the old tried-and-true *Under The Sea* theme. My senior year was some sort of jungle theme, because the backdrop is a leopard skin in the picture of my date Cindy and me. There was a red carpet from the double front doors to the stage where the previous and the newly crowned Homecoming Queens entered with their escorts. Miss Mistletoe walked the carpet at the Holly Ball, as did the King and Queen at the Sweetheart Dance. The Homecoming dance in the tenth grade was when I got my first kiss. I won't say who the girl was, but I was fifteen and she was thirteen. What can I say, at fifteen I got a late start.

At the beginning of my junior year I met a girl who had just moved to Gresham Park from Florida. Her name was Scarlett and she was pretty, funny and smart. We went out a few times before I asked her to the Homecoming dance. On the Saturday before the dance, she stopped by the house while I was not there. She asked my parents to have me give her a call when I got home. She drove a blue Ford Pinto and my mother told me she had a carload of girls with her. She must have had on no makeup, a t-shirt, jeans and her hair tied up, because my father looked at me and said, in not so delicate a manner, that she was not all that attractive. I knew better and blew him off. I went downstairs and

called Scarlett. “What color is your suit?” she asked.
“Brown.”
“Do you have a brown shirt?”
“Yes.”
“I have a brown hot pants suit. Do you mind if I wear hot pants?”
“Uh, no, I don’t mind if you wear hot pants at all.”
“Great! See you Monday at school!”
“See you then.”
I hung up the phone and stood there trying to process what had just happened. I was taking Scarlett to the Homecoming dance and she was wearing hot pants. For a seventeen-year-old boy, this was the stuff dreams were made of. I decided not to tell my parents or anyone else, for that matter.

The evening of the dance I borrowed my mother’s Ford Fairlane and drove over to Scarlett’s house. She walked down the stairs of their split-level house wearing a brown velour vest, a white lace long sleeve blouse, light brown stockings, brown shoes and, of course, brown velour hot pants. She looked absolutely stunning. I pinned her yellow corsage on her vest and she pinned my boutonniere on my jacket lapel. Her mother snapped a few pictures of us and we left to pick up Moon and his girlfriend. We then went back to my house so my mother could take pictures. I’ll never forget walking into the living room with Scarlett on my arm. My father took one look at her and his eyes about bugged out of his head. He couldn't keep from staring at her and kept falling over himself being overly nice to her. At one point I eased over beside him, turned my head and under my breath said, "You still think she's not all that attractive?" "Uh, no," he said and continued staring. He never made mention of any of my girlfriends' physical appearance after that.

As great as the Homecoming Dance was, it paled in comparison to the biggest dance of the year, the Junior-Senior Prom. Prom, like most things, was a lot different back then than it is today. First of all, there were no limos. We all drove our own cars or our parents' cars. Moon and I borrowed his parents' 1968 Chevrolet Impala both years that we went to the Prom. That was as good as a limo to us, because he had a Karmann Ghia and I had a Volkswagen. Yes, couples rode to Prom in Volkswagens, the girls in their big poofy dresses and the boys in their tuxes.

Prom took place in the ballroom of one of the big hotels downtown. The Junior Class always sponsored prom and I was on the committee that selected the band we were hiring to play. We were referred to an agency downtown and spent an afternoon going through the process of looking at eight by ten black and white promo glossies of the bands and listening to demo tapes. It came down to two bands and we ultimately selected a band called Whyrl over one that went by the name of

Mother's Finest. The following year the Junior Class selected Mother's Finest and we were made painfully aware of the mistake we had made the year before. I remember they did a Sly And The Family Stone medley that was incredible. I don't know what ever became of Whyrl, but a couple of years after prom Mother's Finest released an album and achieved just a bit of notoriety.

Mother's Finest may have gone on to make Southern Funk Rock history and it's still cool being able to say they played at our Junior-Senior Prom, but Columbia High School has the distinction of having the ultimate prom band. In 1970 The Allman Brothers Band played at their Junior-Senior. It was held in the gym, presumably because they blew the budget hiring them to play. This was about a year before the *Live At The Fillmore East* album was released and propelled them to superstardom.

Another prom tradition was going out to eat at a fancy restaurant afterwards. There were two restaurants where everyone seemed to go, either the Midnight Sun at Peachtree Center or The Diplomat, which was located on Spring Street. We went to The Diplomat. Bear in mind that we were a bunch of kids from the suburbs on the east side of town and had never eaten in a restaurant anywhere near as fancy as The Diplomat. My first prom I took a girl named Danielle. She was two years younger than me, vivacious, funny, outgoing and absolutely beautiful. We both ordered lobster for dinner. I don't know if Danielle had ever eaten lobster before. I know I hadn't. She was pulling at the meat in the tail with her fork when suddenly the meat broke free and the fork flung it over her shoulder and across the restaurant. She started laughing hysterically. She tried it again and spilled the dish of melted butter on the front of her dress. Again she started laughing hysterically. People were beginning to stare at us. My friend George ordered a steak. George was a big guy who played tackle on the football team. When the waiter brought his steak, George asked for a bottle of ketchup. The waiter stared at him with a look of utter disdain, then left. He returned with the bottle of ketchup and George poured about half of it on the steak. The waiter was horrified and left in a huff.

My senior year I landed a job as a Custodial Engineer for the DeKalb County Board of Education. That meant that I worked on a crew that traveled around to different schools at night, stripping and waxing classroom floors. It was a great job and a lot of fun but the best thing about it was that I got paid about one hundred and seventy-five dollars every two weeks. I thought I was rich and decided to pull out all of the stops and rent the ultimate tuxedo for prom. My date's name was Grace. She was a tall blonde girl who was on the drill team. The polite thing to do in all formal and semi-formal affairs was to find out what color dress your date was wearing and wear a shirt or tie that matched or complimented her dress. Grace's dress was lavender and she wore long white gloves. I went to a men's formal wear shop across from The Varsity called The Tech Shop and rented not only a lavender shirt but also a white tux with a white bow tie, a waistcoat, tails, a top hat and a cane. The top hat was the silk kind that folded flat. You would snap the brim on your wrist and the hat would pop open. We had our pictures made, danced to Mother's Finest, ate dinner at The Diplomat and went to Six Flags the next day.

On Monday I returned the tux to The Tech Shop. I parked in The Varsity parking lot and before I got out of the car, I looked at the top hat folded flat and resting between the two front seats of my Mach 1 and made a decision. I walked into The Tech Shop. "I don't have the hat," I said to the man behind the counter. My nose began to grow. "I left it folded up on the table and got up to dance," I continued. "When I came back to the table, it was gone." I then said, truthfully, "I bought insurance on the tux." He stepped to one side to avoid my nose, which by then was about three feet long, shrugged his shoulders and said, "Give me five dollars." I gave him the five dollars, walked out of the shop, got into my car, popped the hat open, put it on my head and drove away. About six months later I went into McDonald's in Gresham Park and left the top hat in the car, again folded flat, with the windows down. When I came back and got in the car, the hat was gone. That was my first real lesson in karma.

A few years back when we were cleaning out my parents' house and preparing to put it on the market, I found a couple of pictures from the Homecoming Dance and the two from prom. One of the pictures was of Scarlett in her hot pants suit with me holding on to her and smiling from ear to ear. Another was of Grace in her lavender dress and me in my white tux with the tails and top hat. I scanned them and posted them on social media. The picture of Grace and me created quite a buzz. I made the comment when I posted the picture that Grace looked absolutely beautiful, while I, on the other hand, looked absolutely ridiculous. "Hey, we looked good that night!" she said. "You know, Grace," I told her, "I have never again been that dressed up in my life, not even when I got married." And that's the truth. The memories are there. They always will be.

Thrill Hill

There is an old saying, "To be old and wise, you must first be young and stupid." I have the old part down, but I absolutely nailed the young and stupid part. Google young and stupid and you'll get a picture of a fresh-faced me, complete with a Wikipedia article. And nothing proves the depths of my youthful stupidity more than Thrill Hill.

The hill is at the end of a street in East Atlanta. It runs off of a main road and is about half a mile long. I'm not going to divulge the name of the street because I don't want to encourage such behavior, but those that were there in that time and season know exactly where it is.

If any street in the world ever needed speed breakers, it's this one. To make a proper run at Thrill Hill, a daredevil would start on the end off of the main road and give it the gas. There were a few small hills and a stop sign at a three-way intersection right before the big hill. The stop sign was pretty much ignored, especially on a full-speed run. You would hit the crest of the hill at about forty-five miles per hour and your stomach would leap into your throat. You then immediately had to hit the brakes hard, because the street came to a dead end at the intersection with another street about one hundred yards from the crest of the hill. My father first introduced me to Thrill Hill when I was no more than five or six years old. He took me over the top of it in his 1947 Mercury Coupe. Before I came along, he took my older cousins over the hill, too. So I suppose that made Thrill Hill kind of a family tradition.

I took the family tradition to extreme proportions in high school. I remembered the hill from my childhood but did not know exactly where it was located. One of my esteemed secondary education colleagues informed me as to its geographic coordinates. He then took me on a field trip to those selfsame coordinates and over the top of them. The family tradition of Thrill Hill was renewed that day and I pursued it with a vengeance. I would go over Thrill Hill all the time, sometimes circling around and making about five or six passes. I'm sure that there were wrecks on Thrill Hill and I have been told that there was at least one fatality. It's a miracle that it wasn't me. Anyone who happened to have been in my car, laughing and shrieking with fear and glee, I apologize for putting your life in danger. Heaven help us if a car had been coming the other direction over the hill, but that was never taken into consideration.

I had a '71 Pinto that would get airborne going over Thrill Hill. Pintos may have blown up when they were rear ended, but they were designed perfectly for Thrill Hill. I would hit the hill and the car would fly over the crest and come down for a smooth two-point landing with the back tires chirping as they hit the ground. A friend of mine lived in the house at the very end of Thrill Hill. It is a miracle I never ended up in his driveway, garage or back yard. Another friend lived at the very top of the hill. I spent the night at his house a few times and we could hear other scholarly youngsters going over the hill all night long hooting and hollering, their engines roaring and tires screeching.

A good buddy of mine named Stretch owned a green '64 Ford Econoline van. One night a group of us decided to take the van over Thrill Hill. We turned onto Thrill Hill Avenue, Stretch kicked in the other half of the one-barrel carburetor and took the Econoline through the gears using the three-on-the-tree shifter. We lumbered over the hills approaching the big one and sailed through the stop sign. The van chugged up and over the top of the hill and lurched to a halt at the stop sign. We all were laughing hysterically. It wasn't much of a ride, but it didn't matter. Stretch and his green Econoline van had braved Thrill Hill.

Another adventure far less dangerous but equally as thrilling was going to see the Tripping Dogs. The Tripping Dogs were something that you heard about but weren't really sure if it was true. This was how the story went. There was a house on Ward Lake Road below Cedar Grove that was adjacent to a dirt road. If you turned off of Ward Lake Road onto the dirt road and began blowing your horn and blinking your headlights, three dogs would run out in front of the car and start chasing their tails. One night after a Young Life meeting at Cedar Grove Methodist Church, a bunch of us piled into my Pinto and decided to find out once and for all if the Tripping Dogs were truth or rumor. One of the girls in the car knew where the dogs lived and supposedly had seen them. We turned onto Ward Lake Road from Bouldercrest, drove past Puritan Dairy Farm and took a left onto a dirt road beside a large brick house. I immediately began blowing my horn and blinking my lights and sure enough out ran three dogs, terriers or collies of some sort, barking like crazy and chasing their tails in front of the car. I was laughing so hard I almost ran off the road. The dogs began nipping at the tires as I drove slowly past them and headed on down the dirt road toward the Troll Bridge.

The Troll Bridge was a rickety old bridge that ran over a creek and the dirt road. Supposedly a troll lived underneath it. It was very spooky looking but I never saw a troll. Eventually I became brave enough to stop the car on the bridge, roll down my window, blow the horn and taunt the troll. Girls would be screaming in the car and I probably would have soiled myself if a troll or even a nocturnal woodland creature would have emerged from under the bridge. On the way back up the dirt road the Tripping Dogs put on a show again, barking, chasing their tails and nipping at the tires as we drove slowly by, laughing our heads off.

On one of our first dates, Allene and I went to Oakland Cemetery in Atlanta to shoot pictures. Yes, I took a girl to a cemetery on a date. It was what she wanted to do. She got a lot of shots of the sculptures, flowers and architecture. We visited the gravesites of Margaret Mitchell and Bobby Jones. Afterwards, we went across the street to Tin Lizzie's Cantina for lunch and on the way home my in my VW Cabrio, top down and all, we took a detour down Thrill Hill Avenue. I didn't hit the hill full stride as I once would have done, but I did run the stop sign and went over the hill at a pretty good clip. We didn't become airborne but definitely got the sensation. We were no longer old and wise but once again young and stupid. It's a wonder we didn't toss our tacos.

A few years later, we took Allene's grandson Jamie to the Atlanta Botanical Gardens and had lunch at The Varsity. On the way home we decided to take the scenic route through East Atlanta and Gresham Park. As we were leaving East Atlanta and headed toward Gresham Park, Allene looked at me and said, "Let's take him over Thrill Hill." I turned the Sorento onto the avenue and started down toward the big hill. A couple was walking their dog and glared at us. I'm sure that they knew what we were up to. I rolled through the stop sign and hit the gas as we climbed the hill. As we went over, Jamie was in the back seat giggling and laughing. As I took a left and started back up toward the main road, Jamie said,

"Can we go over it again?" I looked at Allene, grinned and said, "Why not?" I took a left on the main road and drove back up to Thrill Hill Avenue. I turned onto it, gave the car the gas and headed toward the smaller hills, the stop sign and the big hill. The memories are there. They always will be.

The Starlight

Before streaming, Netflix, Hulu and Amazon there were movie theaters. NBC introduced *Saturday Night At The Movies* to television in 1961, but the movies aired were usually five or six years old and long past their run in the theaters. To see a current movie, you either went to the theater or the drive-in. We were lucky. We had a drive-in theater right around the corner. It was the Starlight Drive-In, located on Moreland Avenue. Drive-in theaters were plentiful in the second part of the twentieth century and really did not begin to disappear until the late Eighties or early Nineties. Some of the drive-ins in the Atlanta area were the Thunderbird on Jonesboro Road in Forest Park, the Glenwood on Glenwood Road in Decatur, the North 85 Twin at I-85 and Shallowford Road and the Northeast Expressway Drive-In, located down in a hole at the intersection of I-285 and I-85 North. The Thunderbird was under a landing pattern for the Atlanta Airport, which was located a couple of miles to the west and the planes were regularly passing overhead on the final approach with their engines roaring. All of these drive-ins have now gone the way of the dodo, except for the Starlight.

Built in 1949, the Starlight is still thriving today, sporting six screens. People will drive all the way from Paulding County and beyond to the Starlight to take their kids to the drive-in. In the summer the theater hosts a

Drive-In Invasion featuring live music, classic cars and B-movies from the Fifties and Sixties. The Rock and Roll Monster Bash is also featured around Halloween each year showcasing local artists, organizations, vendors and of course, horror movies.

I remember going to the Starlight with my parents when I was a kid. My mother would pop a big container of popcorn. Along with that we would take Cokes, iced tea and my father's thermos of coffee. I remember going with them to see a Doris Day and Rock Hudson movie and the only thing I remember about it was that Rock drove a convertible into a swimming pool full of soapsuds. They also took my cousin Wayne and I to see *The Blue Max* in the mid-Sixties. By then Wayne and I were becoming much too cool to sit in the car with my parents, so we sat in the folding theatre seats on the patio outside the snack bar. The sound was piped over speakers and you didn't have far to walk to the snack bar or the restroom.

Then came the teenage years and, along with them, mild juvenile delinquency. The big thing was to try to sneak into the Starlight for free. I really don't know why, seeing as most of us had part-time jobs and could easily afford to pay for a ticket. Drive-in tickets were about half the price of a conventional theater ticket. We did not think twice about going to a movie theater and paying full admission for both a date and ourselves.

Maybe it was just the challenge, the thrill of the conquest or wanting to see if we could pull it off. Whatever it was, it wasn't limited to my general neighborhood. I once went to the drive-in with my cousin in Fort Pierce, Florida and we went through the same ritual.

The Starlight had secondary exits for both the North and South theaters, so one of the tricks was turning your lights off and driving in through one of the exits and sliding into a space. This was risky. It would only work if you came in about halfway through the first movie and were able to find a parking place immediately. If you had to ride around and look for a space, you were making yourself conspicuous. It also helped if you were driving your parents sedan that was as quiet as a mouse. If you tried to do it in a yellow, jacked-up Fairlane with glass packs, sneaking in quietly and stealthily was not an option, especially after the drive-in began stationing a DeKalb County cop car at each exit.

The age-old, tried-and-true method was to put one or two guys in the trunk. Sneaking into the drive-in in the trunk was strictly a male activity. Under no circumstances did you ever ask a girl to get in the trunk. If you were with a group of guys and girls, it was okay if one or two guys got in the trunk as long as they didn't have dates. If you went to the drive-in with a girl and asked her to get in the trunk, it would most probably be your last date with her or any other girl, once the word got out.

The Get In The Trunk Technique seemed pretty foolproof on paper, until you got into the drive-in. The next step was the Getting Out Of The Trunk Technique. If it was still dusk, things were considerably more difficult. Trying to hide behind the snack bar was dangerous because there was generally too much foot traffic. The easiest way was to park away from cars where you were kind of isolated. The driver would get out, discreetly unlock the trunk and head for the snack bar. The refugees inside would hold the latch to keep the trunk from popping wide open, then open it slowly and just enough to slide out. They would then stay low, go around the car and slide into the back seat. If you popped open the trunk, jumped out, slapped palms and yelled, "Hey, man, we did it!" you may as well have blown an air horn and lit up sparklers.

If you were on the way to or from the snack bar or pulled into the lot and saw a friend's car and the windows were fogged up, you did not approach the car, bang on the window and ask how they were doing. If they were at the drive-in, the windows were fogged up and the sound box that hung on the pole was not attached to the window, it was obvious that they were doing just fine and did not need you checking up on them.

The last time I went to the Starlight was in the late Eighties. A group of us from the neighborhood took the kids to see *Who Framed Roger Rabbit* and *Batman.* We took a grill and lounge chairs. We backed our S-10 Blazer into our spot and opened the rear hatch. To pick up the soundtrack, we tuned the car radio to the frequency designated at the box office. Long gone were the poles with the boxes. We folded down the rear seat and spread out sleeping bags for the kids to lie on and watch the movie. We cooked hamburgers and hot dogs. It was a lot of fun, but it wasn't the same. It seemed too luxurious. It didn't seem like the drive-in.

In the early Two Thousands, friends of ours bought a cabin in Blue Ridge, Georgia. While visiting them there one weekend, they suggested we go to The Swan, a drive-in located in downtown Blue Ridge. Built in the mid-Fifties, The Swan is functional and thriving, like the Starlight. There were strict rules, though. No grills were allowed and all rear hatches had to be closed or tied down. There was a double feature and a mountain fog rolled in. We could hardly see the screen until about halfway through the second movie. The movies we saw were *War Of The Worlds* and *Batman Begins.* So my last two trips to the drive-in I saw two Batman movies. Holy Popcorn! The memories are there. They always will be.

Hambone

I first met Hambone when I was seven years old and he was eight. We played on the same Little League team, the Barons. Our teams were named after the teams in the Southern League. We were the Birmingham Barons and wore black and white, just like the big club. Hambone was our catcher. I played left out, due to the fact that I had never played baseball or any other sport before in my life.

Hambone and I became friends and our parents became good friends as well. I played football for the first time that fall and we were on the same team, the Wasps. He and another kid named Wimpy became my best friends on the team. We called him Wimpy because he loved hamburgers. All kids love hamburgers, but Wimpy took it to another level. In high school, Hambone and Wimpy became best friends. Years after we had all finally grown up, Hambone and Wimpy remained best friends and still see or talk to one another on a daily basis. It's funny how life works out sometimes.

That first season on the Barons turned out to become pivotal in my life and my parents' lives. A kid named Eddie, who was two years older than me, was on the team. His parents and my parents became best friends. Eddie's younger brother was named Herb and Herb became my best friend outside of the neighborhood.

Our families spent holidays together, went to family reunions together and remained lifelong friends even after we had moved to opposite ends of the Metro Atlanta area.

When my cousin Wayne moved to Gresham Park, his next-door neighbor was Hambone. My mother and Hambone's mother were in the same Sunday School class and sat next to each other at Gresham Park Baptist Church for years. I remember vividly my mother calling to me in her Texas twang, "Jimmeee! Ah need ya t' git reddy, weeze a-goin' over to th' Hamziz." My mother's grammar, God Rest Her Soul, was atrocious.

The first zip line I ever rode was in Hambone's back yard. It's actually the only one I've ever ridden, which is maybe why a zip line ride is near the top of the bucket list. Hambone's was nowhere near as sophisticated as the zip lines in the North Georgia Mountains today. It wasn't even called a zip line. Hambone's was called the Shoot-To-Shoot and it consisted of a cable that ran from the top of his tree house on one side of the back yard down to the top of the wooden fence on the opposite side. The cable had a six-inch pulley wheel on it. Hambone had cut a bicycle handlebar, put it through the hole in the pulley and attached handlebar grips to each side. You would hold onto the grips, go off the front of the tree house and ride the pulley down to the fence on the other side of the yard. Ever the entrepreneur,

Hambone bought a roll of tickets from the dime store. He sold them for a quarter apiece and a ticket bought you a ride on the Shoot-To-Shoot. There were a few mid-air falls and a number of crashes into the wooden fence. Nobody was ever seriously injured and we would climb back up the ladder to the tree house for another ticket and another ride on the Shoot-To-Shoot. Hambone would even ride it hanging from his knees. I never tried that myself.

Hambone had the highest threshold of pain of anyone I have ever known in my life. The inevitable childhood cuts, bumps, burns, scrapes and bruises were of no concern to him. In a football game at Gresham Park, he was carrying the ball and took a pretty hard hit on a tackle. In the huddle he realized his mouth was bleeding and took out his mouthpiece. His front tooth was stuck in the hard rubber. Hambone put the mouthpiece back in his mouth and finished the series of downs. He went without a front tooth for years before eventually getting it capped in high school.

During two-a-day football practices one year, we were going through a coverage drill and rotated from one side to the other. When it was my turn, I lined up against Hambone. Friendship went out the window when you were lined up against one another on opposite sides of the ball. I ran my pattern and the throw was a little high. I stretched out to make the catch and Hambone put his helmet right in my side. It knocked the breath out of me, but somehow I made the catch. I ran back gasping and wheezing and handed the ball to Duke. I bent over in line with my hands on my knees, trying to regain the ability to breathe. One of the guys behind me started laughing. A senior captain looked at him and said, "What are you laughing at? He made the catch, didn't he?" The guy quit laughing and I began to breathe normally just as it was my turn to line up and cover a pass pattern.

The morning of the first day of two-a-days that same year, a little black terrier mix dog with brown eyebrows was on the practice field. There was also an empty bottle of Jim Beam bourbon on the field. The little dog was there that afternoon and the next morning. He became our mascot and we named him Jim Beam.

He became part of the team that day and Hambone took him home. Beam went from being a homeless stray to living like a king overnight. He was never fenced and attended every practice. He sat on the sidelines on Friday nights at Panthersville Stadium and rode on the bus with the team to away games. Hambone brought him to school on football Fridays. He went to class with Hambone and had free roam of the gym during the pep rallies. He loved the attention and never acted out, although there was one incident involving a member of the drill team. The Royalettes were performing a routine at a pep rally and Beam must have decided that one backside was shinier than the rest. He jumped up and nipped it and the owner of the backside let out a shriek. She was mortified, to say the least.

Jim Beam was our mascot for that year only. He was mysterious in how he appeared and how he departed. After each game when the team bus returned to the school, we all left for our after-game dates or social gatherings. Hambone took Jim Beam by his house and let him out as he had done all season long. When he came home that night Beam was nowhere to be found. We never saw him again. He showed up the very first day of the season and left on the very last night. Jim Beam was a magical part of not only the football team but also the entire school that season. There are even two pictures of him in the yearbook. One is of him standing on the bench during a football game. In the other he is sitting in class and the teacher is petting him. I hope that he is waiting on The Rainbow Bridge for each and every Warhawk. I know that he is waiting for Hambone.

Hambone loved animals. He had a horse throughout his childhood and teenage years and has owned horses for most of his adult life. One Sunday afternoon I was riding down Bouldercrest Road from East Atlanta and just as I rounded the big curve before Walker, there was a rider on a horse galloping full speed down the road.

The rider was wearing a white Walker football jersey. Then I saw the familiar #32 and realized it was my buddy. I slowed way down so as to not spook the horse. When he slowed from a gallop to a trot I eased around him, stuck my hand out of the open driver's side window and waved. Hambone gave me a thumbs up and we both continued on our way.

As fearless as he was on the football field and on the wrestling mat, Hambone was just as fearless on a pair of water skis. His girlfriend's parents were members of a club called The Gresham Park Boating Club. They would travel to Clark Hill Reservoir in east Georgia for weekends of camping, boating and fun in the sun. Hambone liked to finish off a skiing session with a flourish by jumping outside of the wake, letting go of the rope and riding the skis onto the shore where he would step out of them and walk to the picnic table. The adults warned him against doing that but, as is usually the case with teenage boys, their advice fell on deaf ears. Sure enough, he misjudged his speed on one occasion, hit the beach full speed and went through a thicket of trees before coming out on the beach at the other side. Everyone ran to see if he was okay and he told them that he was fine. What he didn't tell them was that he hurt like crazy but, as he said, "I couldn't let them know that."

A friend of ours named Digger bought a ski boat the

summer after we graduated and we began to take skiing trips to Lake Lanier. They were usually day trips, but on one occasion Digger, Hambone, a guy named Zeke and myself went up on a Friday night. We camped out and skied all day Saturday. Upon arrival on Friday night, we decided to indulge in a little nighttime skiing. We doubled up with two ropes on the back of the boat and Hambone and I were the first two to go. Digger had a spotlight on the boat and while he drove, Zeke kept the spotlight on us skiing. Hambone jumped outside the wake and Zeke followed him with the spotlight. If you have ever been on a pair of water skis in the middle of Lake Lanier when it is pitch dark, you know that it can be pretty unnerving, even if you are eighteen years old, fearless and know everything.

Hambone shares my love of Volkswagens. He had a beige mid-Sixties model Bug he drove in high school. Hambone and the Bug were involved in a fender bender and the front fender was replaced with a blue one. He spray-painted the other fender, the hood and the two front quarter panels blue as well. It looked kind of weird, but when you saw it coming you knew it was Hambone. He now owns two convertible Bugs and a VW bus that is painted psychedelic. It has the Sgt. Pepper's logo on the front and is appropriately called The Magic Bus.

A pillar of Gresham Park, Coach D. of the DeKalb

Yellow Jackets passed away and many people from the community attended his funeral. Hambone drove up from Ft. Myers, Florida and arrived just about the same time as the wrestling coach and backfield football coach at Walker, Coach G. There was lots of hugging, handshakes and laughter. That was what Coach D. would have wanted. At one point there was a group of us standing in a circle. The group included Duke, Hambone, Harry, Coach G., Stan and myself. We all had been on the wrestling team, the football team or both. "Well," somebody said, "here we are. Full circle." We all looked at one another, smiled and laughed. Friendship and brotherhood. The memories are there. They always will be.

Rolling

A high school sport that never made it into the yearbooks, newspapers or morning announcements was rolling. Rolling was an activity that was done off campus, after school hours and was not sanctioned by the state athletic association. It took place under the cover of darkness in front yards throughout the community and involved covering the trees with streams of toilet paper. The basic fundamental was throwing the roll. You would unroll a roll about two feet, then throw it as high as you could into a tree. A perfect throw unrolled on the way up, went over a tree limb and unrolled the rest of the way down. You would then pick up the roll from off of the ground or out of the tree limbs, tear the paper off and throw the roll again. This continued until the supply of rolls was exhausted and the front yard looked like the septic tank had blown up.

I was one of the captains of the rolling team at Walker High School. We didn't get letter jackets or certificates of participation. If letter jackets had been awarded for rolling, there would have been an emblem of a roll of toilet paper in the middle of the crimson "W." We also didn't get to appear at pep rallies or award presentations, although there was a picture in one of the yearbooks of the front of the school when it was rolled.

A typical rolling session usually started with a group of

friends either riding around, gathered at someone's house, attending an evening school function or a sanctioned sporting event. Someone would say, "Hey, let's go rolling!" and the game was on. The next step was to select whose yard you were going to roll. The perfect candidate was someone who was fairly well known and their front yard contained a lot of trees. One of the Walker majorettes was named Mary. Her front yard was full of tall loblolly pines, so it became a frequent target.

After selecting a yard it was time to stock up with supplies, which meant going to Kmart and buying one or two of the bulk packages of toilet paper that contained about thirty rolls. A group of laughing and giggling teenagers going through the checkout line with sixty rolls of toilet paper was usually pretty telling as to what the evening's activity might be. The cashier would either laugh too or look at us with total disdain and disgust. Once the Kmart store manager refused to sell us two packages. Stepping up as captain of the team, I said, "Okay, fine, we'll just go to Big Apple." He sold us the rolls, but I remember having to sign a waiver of some sort.

The best roll thrower I ever knew was my friend Herb. Herb was a pitcher and played quarterback in traditional sports and could launch the roll far and high, unrolling as it moved toward its apex. The roll would sail over one of the top limbs, unroll on the way down and land at his feet. Herb would then pick the roll up, tear it from the tissue streamer and launch another salvo high into the nighttime sky. It was a beautiful sight to behold.

Rolling had to be performed quietly and stealthily, due to the fact that we were high school kids and had curfews, so decorating a yard at three in the morning was not an option. Silence was not the easiest thing to accomplish, especially if you had inexperienced or rookie rollers who would snicker and chortle the whole time. The safest way to approach a yard was to park on the street in front of the house, quietly exit the car, open the packs of toilet paper, place the packs in the middle of the yard and go quickly to work. Depending on the number of throwers involved, a proper rolling session could be completed in ten to twenty minutes. This would also involve covering hedges and bushes if any were available. After finishing, you would quietly climb back in the cars and leave, taking the empty toilet paper plastic bags with you. After all, you didn't want to litter. Once in the safety of the car you could let out with howling laughter, especially after circling the block and riding back by the house to admire your work, with the streams of toilet paper waving in the breeze like Old Glory.

I remember riding with my parents on Sundays to church or to my grandparents' house and passing a yard that had been rolled. My parents would start laughing and my father would slow down so we could admire the handiwork. Occasionally we would pass a yard that I had been involved in decorating, but I never admitted it. One night we rolled my girlfriend Jane's house and the next day we rode by to check it out. She was in the front yard with the garden hose, spraying the trees and pulling the streamers down. I felt guilty, took Moon home, drove back to Jane's house and helped her clean up. It was the least that I could do. At one point she asked, "You didn't do this, did you?" "Me? No," I said, mustering a look of innocence. "Moon and I went to the movies last night." She looked at me suspiciously, but the fact that I was there helping her eventually cleared any doubts that she may have had.

My own yard was rolled one weekend when I was on a Young Life retreat at Awanita Valley in South Carolina. Moon and our buddy Harry led a group of mostly girls in decorating our yard. I know this because my parents stood at the garage door and watched through the window. The next day our neighbor across the street, a retired military officer and the self-appointed neighborhood security guard, knocked on the door and told my father, "I got the tag numbers off the cars of the people who did this to your yard. I looked them up and I know who they are." "So do we," said my father. "It was Moon, Harry and a bunch of girls." My parents also left the toilet paper in the trees so that I could see it when I got home on Sunday. After admiring my friends' handiwork, I went about the task of clearing the streamers from the trees and the yard.

Oddly enough, it was better to roll a yard when the family was home. If they weren't, you ran the risk of them pulling into the driveway and catching you in the act. The closest we ever came to getting caught was the night we decided to roll Coach's yard. There were about seven or eight of us and things were going along smoothly. Herb and I were standing in front of a bedroom window and I whispered to him that I needed another roll. All of a sudden a familiar drawl said through the window, "I'm gonna give y'all about five seconds t'clear outta here and then I'm gonna start shootin' right down th' middle." We all bolted, jumped in the cars and drove away in fear. On Monday morning Herb and I were walking down the hall before school and met Coach coming the other direction. He looked at us and started shaking his head and laughing. We shook our heads and started laughing too. We passed each other without saying a word. He knew. We knew. The memories are there. They always will be.

Arrogant Rascals

Once upon a time, there was a class for juniors and seniors in high school called Driver's Education. Judging by the driving I see on the road today, it needs to be brought back, not just for students but for adults as well. Most all of us at Walker High School and our neighboring institutes of secondary education took Driver's Ed. As a Driver's Ed student, not only could you leave school during the day and go driving around, but also your insurance premium was discounted if you completed the course successfully. Driver's Ed was either a pass-or-fail course. Most students passed. Some of us didn't.

A man named Pickle taught Driver's Ed at Walker. Not Mr. Pickle, just Pickle. The name suited him perfectly. Sour, ornery and country as the day is long, Pickle was one of those teachers that you had to wonder why he ever chose to enter the profession. He had a genuine disdain for teenagers, or "arrogant rascals" as he called us. If you asked him a question he'd look at you and say, "Are you gittin' smart with me?" When calling roll, he would mispronounce students' names. When the students corrected him, he would completely ignore them and mispronounce their names again the next day.

Pickle was a math teacher before they switched him to Driver's Ed. He had a poster on the wall of his classroom of a cartoon car crashed into a tree with a liquor bottle and a bottle of pills beside it. At least once every day he'd point to it and remind us that "Alkyhawl plus drugs equals car again' tree." That was our Driver's Ed version of an algebraic equation.

One of the main strategies of Driver's Ed was scare tactics. You heard rumors about a movie that they showed in the class called *Signal 30.* It was made in 1959 and was the Ohio State Patrol's code name for a fatal accident. Sure enough, Pickle showed us the movie. It was pretty graphic, but it could not compare to the day that a DeKalb County police officer came in with slides of accidents from around the county. They hit home more than *Signal 30* because they were local, more up to date and the officer had been involved in the cleanup of several of the accidents.

At Q&A time after the slide show, I asked the officer, "Is it illegal to drive barefoot?" My father had told me that it was and would have a conniption if I attempted to climb into my car and drive away barefoot. I had asked Pickle once and he just looked at me as if snakes were crawling out of my ears. The officer told me, "No, it is not illegal to drive barefoot, but the fact is that you can apply more pressure to a brake pedal while wearing a shoe." I didn't care about any of that, though. I had my answer and the only thing I cared about was going home and telling my father that a DeKalb County Police Officer had told me that it was perfectly legal to drive barefoot. He looked at me like he didn't believe me but never said anything about it again, thus ending an ongoing disagreement.

After a month or so of classroom work, Driver's Ed began lessons on the road. We drove in pairs with Pickle riding shotgun. I heard that while you were on the road he would point out shrubbery and tell you if it was a male or female bush. I don't know because I never made it to the actual driving portion of Driver's Ed. One afternoon Moon and I were leaving football practice and Pickle was in the school parking lot with a couple of students practicing parallel parking with orange cones. We decided it would be a great idea to moon them. As was always the case, he came up with the idea and I was the one who carried out the plan. We stopped at the top of the parking lot, switched seats and tore past them, blowing the horn with Moon behind the wheel of my '65 Fairlane and me riding shotgun with my Luna Plena hanging out the window and illuminating the early evening sky. The girl who was practicing parking later told me that Pickle started yelling "WHO WUZ THAT, WHO WUZ THAT?" She began laughing so hard that Pickle got mad at her, but he managed to get my tag number and turned me in.

The next morning I was called into the assistant principal's office. Pickle was in the office as well. He described in detail my shameless act of public indecency and told the assistant principal that I was nothing but an arrogant rascal. I was dismissed from Driver's Ed immediately. I got three licks from the assistant principal, not Pickle. I also wasn't allowed to drive to school for a week and had to run countless wind sprints after football practice. As usual, Moon's name never came up. It was, after all, my car and my exposed backside. Miraculously, my parents never found out about it and were spared the shame and humiliation. But Pickle, the assistant principal and the girl who was practicing parallel parking were well aware of the truth. They all knew that I was nothing more than an "arrogant rascal." The memories are there. They always will be.

All Skate

All Skate! Everyone Skate! Everyone, that is, except me. I cannot roller skate. I never have been able to roller skate. I was always able to pretty much play any sport that I wanted to play and do reasonably well, but roller skating was the one thing that was like liver. Try as I might, I could never get it down.

Like a lot of kids, I got a pair of roller skates one year for Christmas. They were the kind that strapped on your US Keds or PF Flyers with leather straps and had a skate key to adjust the length and width. I lived on a big hill, so going down the street was a breeze. It was coming back up that was the problem. I would push and push and never get rolling. So I would sit down on the curb, take the skates off, run back up the hill, strap them back on and fly back down again.

In the mid-Sixties skateboards came along. At first skateboarding was called sidewalk surfing. We didn’t have any sidewalks in our neighborhood, so we surfed the big hill on our street. Like everything else, the boards were a lot different then than they are now. They weren't fancy fiberglass jobs with custom wheels and ball bearings. You cut out a piece of board, took the wheels off of your roller skates and screwed them to the bottom of the board. Then you painted the board up with a racing stripe, a surfer's cross or a Rat Fink decal and it was Surf City! You would ride the board down the hill, pick it up and run back up to the top. As you became more experienced, you would put one foot on the board and push back up the hill using the other foot. This method looked and felt much cooler.

Then, the teenage years came along. The skating rink was a favorite gathering spot for adolescents and the Rainbow Roller Rink on Highway 212 was the one that was in the closest proximity for Walker, Southwest DeKalb and Lithonia High Schools. A friend and I went to Rainbow one Saturday night and I had forgotten the fact that when I attempted to roller skate, I looked like a mule going up a ladder. Besides, I was a kid back then. I was sixteen now and invincible. I played football, for Pete's sake! Surely I could handle something as simple as roller skating.

The guy I went to the rink with could skate like he was on Roller Derby. He was doing spins, skating with two or three girls at a time and never fell. I would fall for no apparent reason and never once attempted a spin. I was doing my best to try and stay upright. The only time I did a spin was when some kid hit me and I did a three-sixty before landing on my butt.

Girls from Walker were laughing and pointing at me. Girls I didn't even know from Southwest DeKalb and Lithonia were laughing and pointing at me. When you are sixteen and girls are laughing and pointing at you, it is traumatic. At least the girls from Southwest DeKalb and Lithonia wouldn't laugh and point at me on Monday morning at school.

A few times a group of us went ice skating at the old Igloo Ice Skating Rink on Roswell Road in North Atlanta. I liked that better because nobody could ice skate, so nobody laughed and pointed at me.

Twenty years later my wife Mary Jane and I visited family in Mississippi for Thanksgiving. Instead of going shopping on Black Friday we all went roller skating. Again, time had blurred the fact that I could not skate. I had learned to water ski my senior year in high school, so surely I would be able to roll around on a pair of skates.

Out on the floor there I was again, looking like Francis The Talking Mule trying to go up a ladder. This time little kids were laughing and pointing at me, even my own eight-year-old daughter who was literally skating circles around me.   My nine-year-old nephew flew on one skate between my legs, causing me to lose my balance. Flailing like an octopus falling out of a tree, I went down on my backside. Even Mary Jane was laughing at me. She could, because she was skating like Tonya without a tire iron. My daughter told me she was going to “teach me how to skate” and tried to help me. But after I body checked the wall, I figured that I had better pack it in before I broke something. And I didn’t mean skating rink property, although that was a distinct possibility. I limped over to the People Who Don't Know How To Skate's Safe Place and watched college football on TV.

As dangerous as I was to myself and to others at the skating rink, I never endured the type of misfortune that befell Allene. She grew up roller skating and was very good at it. Her mom skated in competitions and took Allene and her sisters to the rink one night every week. Skating one night years later with her son, Allene fell and opened a gash in her chin. As she lay on the floor of the rink trying to catch her breath, they put orange cones around her, the pool of blood and then called out, "All Skate! Everyone Skate!" Everyone complied and skated around the cones, leaving Allene dazed, in pain and crumpled on the floor of the rink until they could get her up and to the emergency room for stitches.

One year our nephew had a skating party on his birthday. The rink is right around the corner from the house and there is a hospital nearby. I started thinking again, which is never a good thing. "You've hit a hole-in-one from 125 yards with a 56° sand wedge, for Pete's sake," I told myself. "Surely you can handle roller skating." Then I thought of grandkids, grandmothers and millennial girls laughing and pointing at me. I thought of going to the emergency room and having a broken arm set or an artificial joint installed. I came to my senses and decided to sit on the sidelines and watch. All Skate, Everyone Skate! Everyone, that is, except me. The memories are there. They always will be.

The Mad Hatter

The Mad Hatter was a place that if the walls could talk, oh the stories they could tell! I suppose the walls could actually talk because everybody who went there on a regular basis or even only once has a story to tell about the place.

The Mad Hatter was located in old Underground Atlanta, although it actually was not in Underground per se. It was located in the top of one of the old warehouses at the corner of MLK Jr. Drive and Central Avenue. For about five years, it was the place to be on Wednesday, Friday and Saturday nights. I'm not sure if it was even open any other nights of the week. Fridays and Saturdays there was a one-dollar cover charge, beer was seventy five cents a cup and mixed drinks cost a dollar and a quarter. Wednesday night was Penny Beer Night. We'll get back to Penny Beer Night later.

All the high school alumni in South DeKalb had their hangouts. Walker, Gordon and Cedar Grove's place was Mother's Pub in the back of South DeKalb Mall. Southwest DeKalb's was Bud's Picnic in Chapel Hall shopping center on Wesley Chapel Road at Snapfinger Woods Drive . Columbia and Towers alumni frequented The Keg on Glenwood Road just inside of Columbia Drive. We all visited each other's establishments as well. I'm not sure about other schools' hangouts in the area, but these are the ones I remember.

But everybody went to The Hatter. Often times you would meet up with others at the above-mentioned watering holes before heading downtown as a group. You would walk up two flights of stairs to get to the front door. Three City of Atlanta police officers worked The Mad Hatter. Officer C. carried a pearl handled revolver on his left hip. The other two officers were Officer D. and Officer P. It helped to be on a first-name basis with them. One of the officers would check your ID. You would then pay your cover charge and they would stamp your hand to show you had paid. You were then free to enter and dance the night away.

The ID check was a science all its own. I would hazard a guess that on any given night, probably a third of the crowd in The Hatter was underage. The ink they stamped on your hand took days to wear off, so some would try wetting their hand and then rolling the hand of someone whose hand had already been stamped over their own. This worked sometimes, particularly on the nights they stamped your hand with the number "8," which would transfer correctly if you could get it to work. This method was hit-or-miss. The best method was License Alteration.

I never could figure out why, but they would accept the paper temporary driver's licenses that were issued as valid forms of ID. These were very easy to change. A clean eraser, a sharp number two pencil and a steady hand were all that was needed. You would erase the last digit on the birth year, pencil in the updated digit and suddenly the bearer was two years older and legal. Occasionally the exam date would have to be updated as well, but once you got the hang of it, it was easy pickings. The light was low at the ID checkpoint, and though the officers used flashlights, a decent alteration would get you right in. Since the statute of limitations has probably expired, I suppose it's okay to divulge the fact that I performed License Alteration for a couple of friends. Once it became known that I was proficient at it, I did a few more for five dollars apiece. Five dollars was enough for Penny Beer Night with a dollar left over.

Upon entering you would take a right and the bar was straight ahead against the far wall. The bar wrapped around to the back wall at the left. To the right were tables with a path in the middle leading to the elevated and lighted dance floor. To the left was a supporting post covered with shag carpeting and television screens scrolling through photos taken of the patrons on different nights. Some nights the last thing you wanted was for someone to take your picture. If you continued straight you would come to the door of a small staircase leading to the bathrooms downstairs and a back exit. People would try to sneak in the back exit, but this generally never worked because there was a bouncer with big arms and a small sense of humor stationed down there. You were better off ponying up the cover charge and entering through the front door.

Above the dance floor were the speakers, the DJ and a drum set. A drummer would play along with the music. One night after I arrived at The Hatter, a friend I had not seen in a while came running up to me. He was a professional musician and the last person I ever expected to see in The Mad Hatter. He told me the regular drummer was a friend of his and had asked him to sit in for him that night. I remember how cool it was dancing, looking up and seeing him playing the drums.

While on the dance floor, it was inevitable you were going to hit a slick spot and slip. This was due to spillage from people taking their drinks up on the floor with them. When you hit a slick spot, you would either fall on your butt or appear to be busting a move, depending on your luck.

The carpet in The Hatter was red shag. I don't know if the carpet was ever cleaned. If so, they probably needed HAZMAT suits. From night after night of drinks and who knows what else being spilled onto it, the carpet became so sticky that your platform shoes stuck to it as you tried to walk. The only other place I can compare it to is the Madison Theatre in East Atlanta. I am convinced that the hole in the ozone layer is from when the carpeting in the Madison and The Mad Hatter was removed and burned.

Wednesday night was Penny Beer Night. The cover charge on Wednesdays was the then-astronomical sum of three dollars, but draft beer was a penny apiece. The cups were large green and white paper cups filled with draft beer that I'm convinced had been brewed that morning. You'd put a dollar in the big jar at the bar and you were good for the night. Mixed drinks were a quarter. You could also get an Original Mad Hatter Wine Cooler for a quarter. An Original Mad Hatter Wine Cooler was Boone's Farm Strawberry Hill served over crushed ice in one of the large green and white paper cups. Bottoms up!

I'm not sure how many people would be in The Hatter on any given night, or what the capacity might have been, but things would get tight, very tight. Given the amount of alcohol, cigarettes and polyester in the place, to say it was a fire hazard would be the understatement of the century. And yes, there were fights, lots of them. You can't have that many hormones fueled by cheap beer in tight quarters such as The Mad Hatter and there not be some type of altercation. I managed to avoid getting into one myself but I did witness some pretty good fisticuffs over the years.

On Penny Beer night The Hatter closed at one in the morning. I would leave about midnight or so and head home. I would get a few hours sleep, wake up, shake my head and take a shower. I would throw on my clothes, jump in my Mustang and be at work by eight o'clock, good to go. By lunchtime I was a new man. If I did that now, I'd be in traction for a week.

One particular evening Hambone and I went to the Hatter with our friend Steph. At the end of the evening we were headed out I-20 east toward home in his blue '72 Monte Carlo. Suddenly we struck a pothole and soon heard and felt the unmistakable flapping of a bias-ply tire going flat. We pulled over to the emergency lane and Hambone and I got out of the car. Not just one but both right-side tires were flat as a flitter. The Monte Carlo was a nice car, but like most vehicles had only one spare tire. We discussed our options and Hambone decided to walk to the next exit and call a wrecker. Just about that time, two older gentlemen pulled up and offered their assistance. Seeing the jam we were in, one of them said he had a Chevy wheel and tire at his house and he would sell it to us for four dollars. Times were different back then, but what we did next ranks pretty high on the list of youthful stupidity. For some reason it was decided that Steph and I would ride with the two of them to pick up the tire and Hambone would remain with the car. We rode with these two guys into an Atlanta neighborhood that could only be described as sketchy. We pulled into a driveway, the driver climbed out, went into his garage and brought out a perfectly round and inflated spare tire. He placed it into the trunk and we headed back toward Hambone and the Monte

Carlo. As we approached the car, flashing blue lights of a City of Atlanta police cruiser lit up the surrounding area. The two gentlemen, Steph and I got out of the car. The driver pulled the spare tire out of his trunk and he, his friend and the police officer proceeded to change both tires while Hambone, Steph and I sat on the embankment and watched. They finished and popped the two hubcaps back on. We paid the two gentlemen and thanked them for their kindness. The police officer told us to drive carefully and we all drove away. That simply could not happen now, but it happened back in that time and season. The memories are there. They always will be.

The Grove Revisited

I spent a great portion of my formative years in Cedar Grove. By formative years I am referring to young adulthood, when I was young and knew everything. But they were formative years because I eventually learned a work ethic, values and what it meant to be a responsible adult. This was due in no small part to the people and families I came to know and love in Cedar Grove.

The first person I ever met from Cedar Grove was a boy I went from kindergarten through high school with named Carl. Carl went to Gresham Park Elementary School because his parents would drop Carl off at Davis Kindergarten and Nursery in the mornings on their way to work. The Panda Bus would pick Carl and the rest of us up after school and take us back to the day care center where our parents would pick us up in the afternoon on the way home. Carl's parents continued to do this up until we graduated from grammar school.

Carl became one of my best friends in elementary school. I spent the night at his house a couple of times and he spent the night at mine. Cedar Grove was still a rural community then and Carl's house was almost like a tiny farm. It had a huge front yard and a barn in the back yard. Carl raised chickens and while most of us had paper routes, cut grass or washed cars to earn money, he had an egg route and delivered fresh eggs on his bicycle throughout the Grove.

Like most boys our age, Carl built a fort in his front yard. While most of us would build ours out of pinestraw, leaves and whatever scrap plywood or anything else we could get our hands on, Carl built his between two trees in his front yard. He made it out of actual logs from pine trees that he cut down with an axe. It was open in the back, had two window openings in the front and small tower on each side. They weren't really towers. They were extensions on each side where we could stand and look out the window holes. The other window holes on the fort were low, where we could lie prone or peer out over the top of the wall and protect the house from marauding cars driving up and down the dirt road.

When Carl was about ten years old, his parents put in a swimming pool in the upper part of their back yard, complete with a diving board. This was at a time when backyard swimming pools were few and far between. We would race laps and he taught me how to do a flip off of the diving board.

After elementary school, Carl and I drifted apart. Once in high school, my interests shifted quickly to sports, girls and cars. Carl played clarinet in the marching band and pursued science. He built a lab in the barn behind his house and won an academic scholarship to Georgia Tech. After a year he transferred to the University of

Georgia to study his true passion, horticultural and biological science. While riding his ten-speed bicycle in downtown Athens he was struck and killed by an automobile, a brilliant young mind taken all too early.

On the first day of my senior year at Walker, I walked into American History class and sat down behind a pretty, red-haired girl named Lea. I knew who she was, but we had never really met. We became fast friends. It was a friendship that would last a lifetime. Neither of us were star students by any stretch of the imagination. She would turn around and slap a ruler beside my head on the desk when I had fallen asleep in class. I would pop her bra strap when she had fallen asleep with her head on her desk. We would skip class and go to McDonald's or Dairy Queen. Lea drove a souped-up yellow '69 Camaro and would light up the back tires with the boys in the parking lot.

She and her friend Beverly worked at Tenneco in Gresham Park as Petroleum Transfer Engineers, wearing roller skates and pumping gas. I began to trade regularly at Tenneco and I would hazard a guess I was not the only one. I know my father became a regular customer.

As fate would have it, Moon and Charlie, Lea's brother, were in the same homeroom and became good friends. I had known Charlie throughout high school and even had a couple of classes with him. Any friend of Moon's was a friend of mine, so Charlie and I became buddies about the same time Lea and I became friends.

On Graduation Night at Walker, after exercises had concluded and we were all officially alumni, a group of us guys piled into Charlie's SS396 Chevelle and went to The Pumphouse in old Underground Atlanta, where we drank several pitchers of beer. Back then graduation was on the last day of school, which in 1973 was on a Wednesday. This was because of make-up days due to the infamous '73 Ice Storm. We all had to be at work or, in Charlie's case, a job interview the next morning at the GM plant. He called me later the next day and told me he had passed the job interview, even though he was a little green around the gills. About a week later Lea and I went to Muhlenbrink's Saloon, drank flaming hurricanes and listened to Piano Red. Neither one of us had turned eighteen yet, but the bartender didn't ask for an ID. I guess we looked older and more mature than we actually were.

My parents and I had moved to Spanish Trace Apartments that summer while our new house was being built in Rex. One day Lea brought two of her aunts, Virginia and Angela, to meet me and to swim in the complex's pool. Charlie and Lea's mom was from a large family and their Aunt Virginia was actually Lea's age. Angela was a year younger. Charlie, Lea, nor any of us ever referred to them as Aunt Virginia and Aunt Angela. We only called them by their first names. They lived in Augusta and came to Atlanta often. We would all go to Mother's Pub, The Mad Hatter, Stone Mountain or Arabia Mountain together. When Lea would introduce Virginia and Angela to people as her aunts, the response invariably was, "Your aunts? Don't you mean your cousins?" They never really seemed like Charlie and Lea's aunts or even cousins. They both seemed more like their sisters.

I always had nothing but the utmost respect and admiration for Charlie and Lea's parents. I never referred to them as anything other than "Mr." or "Mrs." Anything else just sounded wrong. Their dad was the hardest working man I have ever known. He could build anything with his hands, including a two-story, four-bedroom brick house with a garage and a heated swimming pool. Their mom was a true southern belle, beautiful, gracious and engaging. She was also quite an athlete, playing softball for Bouldercrest Baptist Church and bowling in a league at Forest Park Lanes. She also drove a Corvette, due to the fact that Mr. H was a supervisor at the General Motors Lakewood Plant. A dyed-in-the-wool GM man, I felt honored that he would allow me to park my Mach 1 and later on my Volkswagen in his driveway. Others were not so lucky. Family members who owned VWs told me they were required to park on the street.

My friendship with Charlie and Lea led to friendships

with other families in The Grove, particularly two brothers named Scot and Neil. They lived in a big brick house on Bouldercrest Road and their house became our gathering place. Moon had moved to Cedar Grove during our senior year at Walker. Our group of friends gathered at Scot and Neil's house for parties, hanging out or meeting up before heading out for the evening or for Sunday rides through the Henry County countryside.

Scot and Neil's parents were two of the most patient parents I have ever known. Scot and Neil had the coolest room in the history of the world that two brothers had the good fortune to share. It was literally a two-room, one-bath efficiency apartment in the basement of their house. You walked down the stairs, took a left at the landing, opened the door and stepped into the living area complete with two sofas, an easy chair, a killer stereo system and the most extensive collection of vinyl I have ever seen in my entire life. You could name any album by any artist and they had at least one copy of it. Separate from the living room was the bedroom with two twin beds and a full bathroom. At the back of the bedroom was the outside door. Their parents didn't mind if you bypassed knocking on the carport door and went down through the back yard to the boys' door. "As long as I see your car in the driveway, I know where you are," their mom would say. Sometimes the stereo or us banging on our guitars would get a little too loud a little too late at night. Three or four bangs on the bedroom floor above would let us know it was time to tone it down.

I was always a Gresham Park boy, but in my late teens and early twenties it sure seemed like I was a Grove boy. I could leave our house in Rex, drive up Highway 42, turn onto Double Bridge Road then head up Bouldercrest Road and be at Scot and Neil's in about fifteen minutes. I liked to say that I lived on the outskirts of Cedar Grove. We even had a few Grove parties at our house in Rex.

Whenever anyone's parents went out of town, a Grove party was on. They were never too wild or loud, although once at Charlie and Lea's a few other Grove boys who were actual musicians showed up with their equipment. I had just bought a used set of Premiere drums. I had no clue how to play the drums but loaded them up in my Volkswagen and headed for Charlie and Lea's house. Scot, who was an excellent drummer, sat in with the others and we had a weekend jam session. Ever mindful of the neighbors, Charlie pulled the plug at eleven o'clock each night and we resumed the session the following afternoon.

We were always mindful of the host or hostess's house and always made it a point to help with the cleanup afterwards to insure that the house was just as it had been when our parents had left. If a guest who was not a member of our core group became too loud or too rowdy they were politely asked to leave. Sometimes they were asked not so politely.

One year on the week between Christmas and New Year's Scot and Neil's parents went to Gatlinburg for a few days. We gathered at seven o'clock on Saturday night for our usual Grove get-together. Around nine o'clock the phone rang. It was Scot and Neil's younger brother David and he told Scot, "We've stopped for gas. I wanted to let y'all know that the roads into Gatlinburg are iced over and closed. We're just north of Marietta and will be home in a little over an hour." We all went into warp speed cleaning mode with Lea and Beverly in charge and leading the way. Within forty-five minutes the house was spotless and we were headed toward Manuel's Tavern to continue the festivities. The next day we all shook David's hand and thanked him for giving us the heads up.

Scot and Neil are gone now, two brothers and friends who like so many others were called home way too soon. Their parents are also gone, as are Lea and Charlie's. Their dad's was the biggest shock. He was larger than life and passed away suddenly at the age of seventy three. "If Mr. H is gone," I told Lea at the funeral, "it means that none of us are safe."

I recently had the honor of doing a composite pencil drawing of Scot and Neil's family. David, his wife Terri and younger sister Wendy each sent a package of family photos for reference. As I looked through the pictures a flood of memories came back and the tears began to flow. After gathering my emotions I sat down at the easel and although I had not done a pencil drawing in over thirty years, the lead began to move smoothly and easily over the paper. The memories are there. They always will be.

Homecoming

"I want you to take me down the route the homecoming parade followed," said Allene. We were planning on having lunch the following day with Mr. A, my senior English and Literature teacher. I had not seen him since graduation in 1973 and was very excited and a little nervous. "Sure," I said. "You mean the whole route?" "Yes, the whole route," she replied.

The next morning we left Conyers and headed up I-20 toward Gresham Park. "Why are we going this way?" she asked. "I figured we would go through Gresham Park and pick up the route at the old ballpark," I said. We got off at the Flat Shoals Road exit. The intersection had been re-configured sometime in the Nineties. Now, instead of taking a left and then a right at Brannen Road, we went straight across Flat Shoals, turned left onto Gresham Road and crossed the bridge over I-20. As we drove through the main drag of Gresham Park, the lyrics and tune of Bruce Springsteen's *My Hometown* went through my mind.

I crossed the creek at the bottom of Gresham Road and turned into what was once the parking lot for the Major League field and got a lump in my throat. It is an empty field now, but I could still see the fences, the bleachers and the concession stand, hear the sounds and catch the scents of the old ballpark. "Everybody in the parade gathered here," I said. "This parking lot would be full of floats, cars and people." I drove through the parking lot and started up the road behind what was once the outfield of the Babe Ruth field and stopped about halfway up the hill. "This is where the parade started," I said to Allene. "This is right where you were sitting on the top of the backseat in that '66 Ford Galaxie convertible." "I wish I knew whose car that was that Daddy was driving," she said. "It probably belonged to somebody he worked with," I said. "Yes," she said, "that must have been it."

I eased up to the stop sign at the top of the hill and turned left onto Clifton Church Road. "The parade came up this way and turned here," I said, turning onto Clifton Springs Way. "That's the old Southern Bell building!" Allene exclaimed, pointing at the familiar windowless, one-story brick building. Her father was a Southern Bell man. "Do you think AT&T still uses it?" she asked. There was an AT&T trucked parked on Weslock Circle in front of the building. "Well, I guess they still use it," she laughed. I stopped at the stop sign and looked at what used to be Clifton Springs. "You can still see parts of the old golf course," I said. "That was the third green and there was the fourth tee." I took a right and started down Clifton Springs Road. "The whole road was lined with people," I said. "The band and the drill team marched all the way from Gresham Park to the stadium."

"How do you remember all this? Did you get to see any of it?"
"Just all the people along the road. Our bus came down the route before the parade. We were at the stadium and in the locker room about the time the parade started leaving the ballpark."

We continued down Clifton Springs Road and crossed the bridge over I-285. "This sure was a long way for the band and the drill team to march," said Allene. "Yes, it was," I laughed. "Think of the poor tuba players. But we were all a lot younger back then." We rounded the last curve and started down the hill toward Panthersville Stadium. As we approached the stadium and drove past it, I couldn't believe my eyes. There was a football game going on! I pulled into the back parking lot and turned around. I started back up the hill, stopped at the main entrance and flipped on the turn signal. "What are you doing?" asked Allene.
"I'm going in."
"To the stadium?"
"No, just the parking lot."
"What if they won't let us in?"
"Then we'll leave. The worst that can happen is they'll tell us to get out."
I turned into the lot and all of a sudden it was game day again. It was an absolutely perfect September morning and I was taken back forty-plus years. I could feel the excitement, the anticipation and the adrenaline. "It must

be a JV game," I said. "The varsity games are always on Friday nights." We drove slowly through the parking lot, past parents and families parking their cars and filing into the stadium. We turned around at the circle at the end of the lot, drove slowly past the team buses, by the home team locker room and up toward Clifton Springs Road. "Boy, this brings back a lot of memories," I said. "The old stadium looks good." "Yes, it does," Allene replied. "It's clean. They've certainly put a lot of money into it," I said, looking at the new turf on the field. We turned left and headed back up Clifton Springs Road to Mr. A's house on Clifton Church Road.

Mr. A opened the door to his house and we gave each other a big hug. He taught English at Walker and McNair High Schools for thirty years and influenced countless young lives. Though I did not realize it in my youth, he instilled in me a lifelong love for literature. He and Allene had never met formally, although they remembered each other. Mr. A's first year of teaching at Walker was Allene's senior year. The two of them hit it off immediately and got along famously. He gave us the tour of his home and his garden. He took us downstairs and showed us his workshop and his impressive library. There was a series of shelves along one wall of his basement containing hundreds of books. He told us that he collected the books from when they were either purged or released from the library. It was the most incredible personal collection of books I had ever seen.

We went back upstairs, talked about Walker and the old days for a while and then headed out for lunch at Little Azio in East Atlanta. Mr. A drove and we took the scenic route. We rode through Gresham Park and past the house where he grew up on Mary Lou Lane. A few doors up we stopped in front of our friend Chappy's house. Incredibly, her house still looks exactly the same as when she lived there. I halfway expected her to walk out the door and wave at us.

We reached the intersection of Mary Lou Lane and Rollingwood Lane and Mr. A asked where I had lived. I told him to take a right onto Rollingwood. We crossed Boulderview Drive and started down the hill, past the spot where I went over the handlebars of my bicycle and down the street on my chin at ten years old. "I lived right here," I said and we stopped in front of my house. I was not prepared for what I saw. The last time Allene and I rode by the house it still looked to be in fairly decent shape. That was not the case anymore. Kudzu covered the yard, parts of the gutters were missing or hanging, iron bars covered the windows, the yard was dirt, paint was peeling from the wooden shutters and a sign in front of the garage door warned me that if I came in the yard I would be shot. That pretty much erased any inkling of desire that I may have had to knock on the door and ask for a tour. I asked Mr. A to give me a minute or two. I stared at the house and the emotion welled up in my throat. I could not quit thinking about the house I had lived in for fourteen years, the way my parents had kept and maintained it and what it looked like now. My heart was broken. We moved on up the hill, turned left on Flintwood and headed toward East Atlanta.

We had a wonderful lunch, continued to reminisce and Allene marveled at the places and details we remembered. Upon leaving, we headed south on Moreland Avenue and turned onto Sky Haven Road. We drove slowly past the empty lot where Sky Haven School, the elementary school Allene had attended, had once sat. We then headed down Ripplewater Drive, turned left onto Eastland Road and drove to the house where she grew up. The little white house still looked good, the shutters were still painted black. The roof over the front porch was gone and a tall wooden fence had been erected around the concrete back patio. Allene's dad's old garage was still out back and appeared to be in good shape.

We drove back down Bouldercrest Road and turned into McNair High School, formerly known as Walker High. We rode around the campus and it was clean and impressive, I have to admit. Mr. A pointed out different aspects of the school and corrected a former observation I had made. The old Walker gymnasium is still the gymnasium. The new building built on the spot that was once the baseball field is the performing arts center.

We finally headed back to Mr. A's house. Once there, he pulled out his collection of yearbooks. He had one from every year he had taught at both Walker and McNair. It was fascinating to look through them, particularly the ones from the years after I had graduated. It was fun to see how life went on after the class of '73 and seeing folks with whom I had been friends while they were underclassmen as seniors.

Mr. A did something back in the day that I have never heard of a teacher doing before or since. He wrote every one of the seniors that had been in his classes a personal letter after graduation. I remember receiving mine and what an impression it made on me, even at eighteen years old. I kept it for a number of years, but it eventually was lost in the move from my parents' house to a place of my own. He pulled a letter out of one of the yearbooks and showed it to us. It was addressed to a girl who had graduated in 1976 and had been returned to him marked as no one at the address. I told him that I was friends with her on social media and could mail the letter to her. He agreed and the next day I sent the young lady a private message. I told her I had visited Mr. A and had the letter. She wrote back and said that her father had passed away two days after graduation and that she, her mom and sister had moved in with her grandmother. That was why the letter was returned. I put it in the mail the next day and forty-two years after Graduation Day, she received her letter from Mr. A.

Allene and I stayed until almost dark and finally decided that we had better get home and tend to Tilley, our whippet. She had been alone all day and undoubtedly was convinced that we had abandoned her. We both hugged Mr. A and thanked him for being such a gracious host. He and I have talked several times since and have exchanged books and ideas. He is truly a gentleman, a scholar, a friend and a mentor.

Several weeks after our visit I went to the mailbox and pulled out an envelope from Amazon. I could tell that it was a book, but it was puzzling because I had not ordered a book recently. I took the package into my studio, opened it up and pulled out a copy of *Brighton Rock* by Graham Greene. It was a book that we read in Mr. A's class. I had asked him when we were visiting if he had a copy in his library and told him that I would like to read it again. He said that he had a copy but would have to find it. I thumbed through the book, laughed, then called Mr. A and thanked him. Forty-five years later, my teacher was still giving me reading assignments. The memories are there. They always will be.

Epilogue

It was a perfect fall afternoon, cool, crisp and not a cloud in the sky. I sat on the top step and watched the birds on the feeders. They were full of cardinals, both male and female. There would be more in to feed at dusk. I heard two Blue Jays bantering with their familiar call and looked out over the creek and into the woods beyond the fence. I thought of the creek behind and the woods beside our house in Gresham Park. They were filled with Blue Jays then and over the years I have come to love hearing their call. I have always felt an affinity for Blue Jays. They remind me of the days of my youth when the biggest stress and worry in my life was math homework.

The woods on Rollingwood are gone now, as are most certainly the Blue Jays. Someone told me once that the West Nile virus had wiped out a large population of the jays. That made me sad, because I had noticed that for a long time I not heard or seen any in the back yard. The population is now rebounding and there are several jays whose habitat is the woodlands of our back yard and beyond.

We have an abundance of Cardinals in our yard and woods. That is good. I know the symbolism of the Cardinal, but to me they also symbolize something more. I have come to think of life as the seasons. Childhood is the spring, the summer is the time of youth and early adulthood, early and late middle age is the fall and the senior years are the winter years. I am in the fall of my time with the winter years are rapidly approaching. The Cardinals symbolize the winter, their coats blazing red, brown and gold against the white backdrop of snow.

And so the Cardinals of the fall and the winter of this time and season have replaced the Blue Jays, the symbol of the place and time of the spring and summer of my youth. As we age, we come to realize that not only each season, but also each day is a gift for which to be thankful. I am also thankful to have crossed paths and shared life with people who had such a profound influence on my life. A few have been mentioned in these pages.

The Sixties and the Seventies were far from idyllic. There was social upheaval, an unpopular, politically-based war halfway around the world that cost millions of young Americans their lives. There were presidential assassinations and resignations. There were riots and there was the Cold War.

But there were also times of peace and prosperity and growth. And it saddens me that there are generations now and to come that will never know that place and time in their lives. They will never know what it was like to attend public school and feel safe. They will, for the most part, never be able to play outside all day until dark, to walk or ride their bike to school or the store. They will never learn to try and to fail, then keep trying until they succeed. The world is literally at their fingertips, with a touch and a swipe on a phone or a pad. I will be the first to acknowledge that technology is great, but a lot has been lost along the way.

A large portion of them will never learn to write cursive. They will never have a pen pal. They will never write a letter to a girl or boy they met on summer vacation and anxiously check the mailbox every day, waiting for a response. They will never subscribe to comic books or Mad magazine. A host of them will probably never go to a library. They will never play Army and most certainly never play Cowboys and Indians.

I am thankful that we were lucky and blessed enough to have lived where and when we grew up. It was a place and a time and a time and a season where we laughed. We cried. We lived. We died. We won. We lost. We experienced joy. We experienced heartbreak. We worked. We played. We had agreements. We had fights. We were praised. We were punished. We learned firsthand to live life. The memories are there. They always will be.

Made in the USA
Columbia, SC
16 March 2019